The Endless Day:
The Political Economy of Women and Work

The Endless Day:
The Political Economy of Women and Work

Bettina Berch
Barnard College
Columbia University

Harcourt Brace Jovanovich, Inc.
New York   San Diego   Chicago   San Francisco   Atlanta
London   Sydney   Toronto

To Mollie and Julian Berch

Printed in the United States of America
Library of Congress Catalog Card Number: 81-85461
ISBN: 0-15-517950-0

PHOTO CREDITS

p. 1: United Press International; p. 23: Brown Brothers; p. 37: Brown Brothers; p. 53: © Randolph Falk/Jeroboam, Inc.; p. 69: © Peter Southwick/Stock, Boston; p. 89: Brown Brothers; p. 107: © Frank Siteman/Jeroboam, Inc.; p. 119: The Bettmann Archive, Inc.; p. 141: © Rose Skytta/Jeroboam, Inc.; p. 159: © Elizabeth Hamlin/Stock, Boston; p. 173: © 1980 Dennis Brack from Black Star; p. 197: © Kent Reno/Jeroboam, Inc.

Preface

This is not a self-help book. You will not learn how to succeed in business without really trying. You will not learn how to dress for success, how to get yours, or even how to convert your bank account into a tax shelter. This book is not about that media phantom, Ms. Horatia Alger, who is moving from the steno pool to the board room with a little luck and lots of hard work. There are enough of these fairy tales already. Neither is this some arcane treatise written by one economist for a lot of other economists about the costs and benefits of discrimination against women. There are enough of those, too.

The point of this book is to explain to you how our economic system in America operates and how it structures the economic life of women. Some may not agree with the idea that a free enterprise economy structures anyone's life, arguing that men and women are free to do what they please. Yet the subtlety of the free market should never be underestimated. Behind the *appearance* of free choice, the market uses *economic incentives* to steer us in certain directions. Relative wage changes signal to us to change jobs, new tax rules encourage us to enter or leave paid legal employment, child care allowances or tax credits may encourage us to have babies earlier, and so forth.

Once we understand that this "market system" induces us to act in certain ways by offering economic incentives, we begin to realize that we need a lot more information about how this economic system is structured and how it structures the position of women. Only when we understand how these signals are supposed to operate can we ever transcend them to engage in the struggle for self-determination. This, after all, must be the meaning of a women's movement: to struggle to be the subjects and not the objects of history.

I will try to make clear how the economic system approaches women's labor: where and how it offers choices, and where choice is denied. In the first three chapters of the book, we will explore what women's work really is and how essential it was and is to our economy. Chapters 4 and 5 will focus on women's labor market work. In these chapters we will examine the conventional theories about why women are paid less and have the worst jobs,

v

and then look at some more convincing alternative explanations. In Chapter 6 we will examine housework: what it is, why it is so necessary to the economy, and why it still requires so much time and effort. We shall go on in Chapter 7 to study women's work in bearing and raising children, the future labor force of our country. We will look not only at the direct costs of childbearing, but also at the indirect, hidden costs. Having examined the economically productive uses of women's labor, in market work, housework, and child-bearing work, we will then see in Chapters 8, 9 and 10, how the economic environment (government, business and the unions) responds to women. We will examine how to compare the diverse situations of women worldwide and try to draw some useful conclusions about the prerequisites for progress for women. In the final chapter, we shall look into the future a bit. Drawing on our previous analyses of women's labor, we can sketch out the developments we might reasonably expect to see in the next few decades.

Women's labor is extremely complex, since it has three productive uses—in the market, in housework, and in childbearing. Because all three are necessary for our economic system to function, various laws and customs have been instituted over the years to ensure an adequate supply of labor for each use. When the birthrate declines, for example, society tries to move women out of the labor force and into the home. During war years, however, women have been told to do less housework and child rearing so they can take production jobs. (When the war ends, women are told to leave these jobs and have babies instead.) While for society women's labor has three productive uses, for women themselves this can be a triple burden: three jobs, and less than one wage (since women still do not receive equal pay in the market-place). If more women can realize that this triple burden is a problem of being overworked, rather than a matter of psycho-social roles, then some long-term relief may yet be in sight.

Before you dig into the text, allow me to salute some friends who have helped me. For my first formal training in women's studies, I must thank Dr. Annette Baxter, who has continued to support my work over the years. In the same breath, let me express my gratitude to my students at Barnard, who have been such a creative audience for my ideas. My thanks also to the Women's Center at Barnard, and to the director, Jane Gould, for the use of their excellent research resources. In addition, let me thank Alice Amsden for her help with the title, Marina Rabinovich and Monica Blagrove for their typing assistance, and Dr. Elyce Rotella, Professor Patricia Huckle, and Professor Janet Kohen for their critical comments. I am grateful to Steve Dowling and Jane Ford at Harcourt Brace Jovanovich for supporting this project and to Susan Collette for her editorial work. And finally, my warmest thanks to Robby Guttmann, who argued with me over most of the contents of this book—but who also made sure I wrote it.

Bettina Berch

Contents

9   The Business World and Working Women

10   The Trade Unions and Working Women

What Is Women's Work?

Why Are Women Workers Called "Secondary"?

Newspapers and television reports—even "economic experts"—are fond of referring to women as secondary wage-earners. This term expresses an underlying assumption that women workers are not as necessary or as natural as male workers. The "new woman worker" is the subject of many articles and analyses. The popular press is full of articles with doubting titles, such as "Are Women Workers Here to Stay?" or "The Two-Paycheck Marriage: How Long Will It Last?"

The alleged decline of family values and female virtue that has resulted from women's entry into the paid labor force is the topic of many of these journalistic forays. The following is a typical remark from one of the "experts": "The whole phenomenon of the dual career couple has exacted a psychic toll and erosion of the traditional family structure. The fallout of this eruption has left a large set of individuals without support networks, leaving them alienated and often dysfunctional."[1] When women have careers, the family is stressed, workers become unhappy, and "when workers are unhappy with home life they do not produce effectively ... our industrial system is jeopardized."[2] This particular columnist (an academic guidance counselor) does not specify whether it is only women with

3

careers rather than women with mere *jobs* that threaten the productivity of our economy, but the basic implication is clear: the "new woman worker" is not only unnatural, but even dangerous to our socio-economic system.

Government statisticians have for a long time found the concept of working women awkward. Since it has been considered abnormal for women to hold jobs, women have not been included in the definition of the permanent, "real" labor force. Thus, when women cannot find jobs, they are not necessarily categorized as unemployed, a state of affairs that tends to lower—artificially—the unemployment statistics.

This myth of the woman worker as less permanent, less typical, and less real is extremely pervasive, even if there is no logical reason for it. Yet we can no longer afford such an inaccurate view of the reality of women's work. To understand women's actual position in the economy requires an examination of some rather dry charts, tables, and statistics. But have patience: the insights from these data are far from dry.

The economists' system of tabulating the economically productive work that takes place in an economy utilizes a set of national income accounts collectively called the gross national product (the GNP). The GNP is the economists' best estimate of the total quantity of legal, paid work performed in the economy in any given year. Our first task, therefore, is to locate women's work in the GNP accounts, which means, in effect, identifying the *number* of women in the paid labor force and the typical sectors of the economy where women usually work. A close look at Table 1-1 should destroy the myth that most women are still full-time homemakers. The table shows the labor force participation rates of men and women in the United States defined as the percentage of the total noninstitutional population that is in the labor force.

Although the male labor force participation rates used to be much higher than the female rates (87% for males in the 1950s compared with about 34% for females), men's participation rates have declined over time, while women's rates have steadily increased. By 1978, male labor force participation had declined to 78.4%, while the women's rate had increased to 50.1%. Since then, women's labor force participation rates have continued to increase: data for June 1980 indicate that 51.4% of the female population is in the labor force. Black women's participation rates are even higher: 52.5% of adult black women were in the labor force in June 1980.[3] With over half of the adult women in the United States in the labor force (during a non-wartime period), the old stereotype of women as full-time homemakers can be discarded.

TABLE 1-1
Participation in the Labor Force: 16 Years of Age and Older
(as a Percentage of the Noninstitutional Population in the
United States)

Year	Male	Female
1947	86.8	31.8
1948	87.0	32.7
1949	86.9	33.2
1950	86.8	33.9
1955	86.2	35.7
1960	84.0	37.8
1965	81.5	39.3
1966	81.4	40.3
1967	81.5	41.2
1968	81.2	41.6
1969	80.9	42.7
1970	80.6	43.4
1971	80.0	43.4
1972	79.7	43.9
1973	79.5	44.7
1974	79.4	45.7
1975	78.5	46.4
1976	78.1	47.4
1977	78.3	48.5
1978	78.4	50.1
June 1979	—	50.7
June 1980	—	51.4

Sources: 1947–78 Employment and Training Report of the President, 1979, Table A-1; 1979–80 Bureau of Labor Statistics Report 611, 1980.

Furthermore, as male labor force participation has ebbed slightly and women's participation risen over time, the *proportion* of women workers in the labor force has increased. As can be seen in Figure 1-1, the labor force has become proportionately "more female" over time, so that women currently make up almost 40% of the civilian labor force. Having seen this rise in female labor force participation, we might now want to know more about what types of women have been entering paid employment. Are they the older women, the middle-aged, or the teenagers?

Figure 1-2 graphs the average participation rates for various age groups in selected years. While it is clear that today more women of all ages are in the labor force, you can also see that the 1950 and 1960 graphs shift upward from the 1940 graph on the older end, while the 1970s graphs shift upward more on the younger end. In other words, growth in women's labor force participation was fueled by the more

FIGURE 1-1
Proportion of Women in the Civilian Labor Force

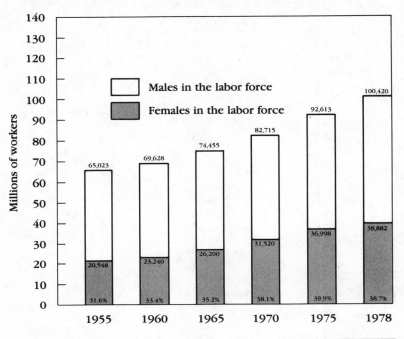

Source: Employment and Training Report of the President, 1979, Table A-1.

mature women (the 45–64-year olds) in the earlier decades and by the younger women (16–34-year olds) in the 1970s. Still, according to 1980 data, the prime female age group for labor force work is the 20–24-year olds: 68.4% of these women are currently in the paid labor force.

These statistics do not *explain* women's labor force participation; they only describe it. To understand more about why older or younger women are entering the labor force, we need information about the family status of women workers. Rarely considered an important variable determining male labor force participation, marital status is an important indicator of women's labor force participation, as a look at Figure 1-3 reveals. While single women and widowed, divorced, or separated women have historically shown high

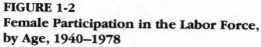

FIGURE 1-2
Female Participation in the Labor Force,
by Age, 1940–1978

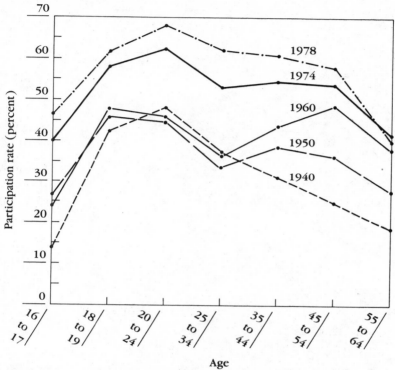

Source: Employment and Training Report of the President, 1979, Table A-2.

labor force participation rates, the steady increase of married women's labor force participation has been dramatic. By June 1980, close to 50% (48.9%) of married women living with their husbands present were in the labor force.[4] What accounts for this steady increase? The trend becomes even more mysterious when we consider that many of these women must be mothers of young children.

The graphs in Figure 1-4 record the labor force participation rates of married mothers of pre-school children (under 6 years old), married mothers of school-age children (6–17 years old), and married women without any children under 18 years of age. In spite of

FIGURE 1-3
**Growth of Women's Labor Force Participation Over Time,
by Marital Status**

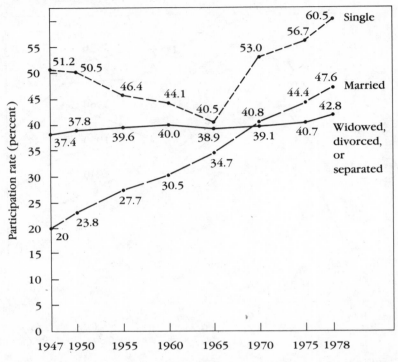

Source: Employment and Training Report of the President, 1979. Table B-1.

the shortage of day care facilities in America, the rising labor force participation of married mothers of pre-school children has been phenomenal. These charts lead us to a major reason why women work: like everyone else, women work in order to eat (and with small children, the need to work is even greater). Add to this a recent statistic: the average American married-couple family with only the husband as income earner lost 6.9% in real (inflation-adjusted) earnings from 1979 to 1980.[5] As will be clear when we examine women's earnings, even if working wives do not earn as much as their husbands, they may have to enter the labor force in order to stem the decline of their family's purchasing power. Women who are supporting families with no husband present are even more likely to be

FIGURE 1-4
Labor Force Participation Rates:
Married Women, Husband Present

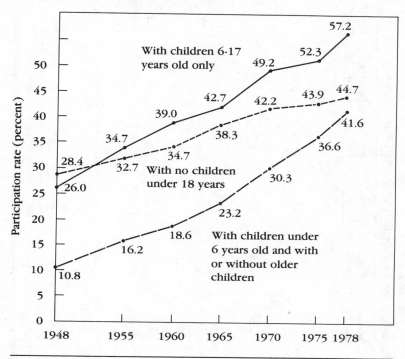

Source: Employment and Training Report of the President, 1979, Table B-4.

in the labor force (58%), and they too experienced a fall (2.8%) in their already-low real earnings in 1980.[6]

The labor force participation patterns of women of different ethnic backgrounds can also be examined. A look at Table 1-2 reveals different participation rates for different groups of women. Filipino-American women exhibit the highest labor force participation rate (55.2%) and Puerto Rican women show the lowest (31.6%), which corresponds also to the rates for married women of these groups. The differences among the various groups can be attributed to different prevailing cultural patterns and to regional and educational differences. Differing child care responsibilities are also a contributing factor.

TABLE 1-2
Women's Labor Force Participation by Ethnic Group and Other Factors

	White American	Black American	Mexican-American	Puerto Rican	Cuban-American	American Indian	Japanese-American	Chinese-American	Filipino-American
Labor force participation rate									
All adult women (percent)	40.6	47.5	36.4	31.6	51.0	35.3	49.4	49.2	55.2
Married women only (percent)	44	48	29	28	49	36	51	48	46
Average family size	3.57	4.15	4.64	4.15	3.74	4.46	3.67	4.01	4.23
Married-couple families with at least 1 child below 6 years of age (percent)	27	32	46	45	30	40	37	33	42
Female-headed families with at least 1 child below 6 years of age (percent)	17	30	30	46	16	32	24	12	39
Median income	$3,738	$2,041	$1,892	$2,938	$2,825	$1,697	$3,236	$2,686	$3,513
Women over 25 who are high school graduates (percent)	54.5	31.4	24.2	23.4	43.9	33.3	68.8	57.8	54.7
Median number of years of school for women over 25	12.1	9.8	8.1	8.7	10.3	9.8	12.5	12.4	12.2

Source: E. Almquist and J. Wehrle-Einhorn, "Doubly Disadvantaged: Minority Women in the Labor Force," *in* A. Stromberg and S. Harkess, *Women Working,* 1978, p. 67.

The Sectoral Distribution of Women Workers in the U.S. Economy

Our statistics, then, show us that women are indeed in the labor force, and in growing proportions as time goes on. We can now move on to the more complicated question of *where* women are located in the labor force. Are they randomly distributed among the various occupations? While even casual empiricism would remind us that women are more typically in certain fields than in others, we need to examine the data more closely to develop a more precise picture of women's employment.

For a historical perspective on the matter, refer to Table 1-3, which ranks the top 10 women's occupations for the past 100 years. Note that it is only recently that the category "domestic servants" has dropped to the bottom of the chart and "stenographers, typists, and secretaries" has risen to the number-one occupation.

A more standard breakdown of occupational sectors is shown in Table 1-4, with current data on women's participation in each sector. From the first column of the table, it is clear that over half of all employed women are in clerical or service work. You might think that this is not so odd. Could it just reflect the fact that our entire economy has moved away from its earlier concentration on primary and secondary work (raw materials extraction and basic manufacturing) and into tertiary or service sector work? As the overall economy has shifted into more service sector work, might we naturally expect more women workers to be employed in these sectors than in any other sectors? Perhaps. But look at the second column of Table 1-4, which shows the percentage of workers that are female for each sector. Close to 80% of all clerical workers are female, and roughly 63% of all service workers are women. The percentages of female managers and craft workers, on the other hand, are rather low. You might wonder what is wrong with such disproportionate concentrations of women in certain job categories. The distributions might mean that women managers or construction workers have a rough time on the job, or that those male secretaries get a lot of stares. This, however, is not the whole problem. As the figures in the third column of Table 1-4 show, women workers are disproportionately concentrated in the low-paying job sectors and male workers are predominant in the high-paying sectors. Furthermore, as the fourth column of data reveals, women's median earnings in every sector are much less than the earnings of their male counterparts. So not only is, say, service work a low-paid field, but on average, women in this field

TABLE 1-3
The Leading 10 Occupations of Women Workers 1870–1970

	1870	1880	1890	1900	1910	1920	1930	1940	1950	1960	1970
1	Domestic servants	Domestic servants	Servants	Servants	Other servants	Other servants	Other servants and other domestic and personal servants	Servants (private family)	Stenographers, typists and secretaries	Stenographers, typists and secretaries	Secretaries
2	Agricultural laborers	Agricultural laborers	Agricultural laborers	Farm laborers (family members)	Farm laborers (home farm)	Teachers (school)	Teachers (school)	Stenographers, typists and secretaries	Other clerical workers	Other clerical workers	Sales clerks (retail trade)
3	Tailoresses and seamstresses	Milliners, dressmakers and seamstresses	Dressmakers	Dressmakers	Laundresses (not in laundry)	Farm laborers (home farm)	Stenographers and typists	Teachers (not elsewhere classified)	Saleswomen	Private household workers	Bookkeepers
4	Milliners and dress and mantua makers	Teachers and scientific persons	Teachers	Teachers	Teachers (school)	Stenographers and typists	Other clerks (except clerks in stores)	Clerical and kindred workers (not elsewhere classified)	Private household workers	Saleswomen	Teachers (elementary school)
5	Teachers (not specified)	Laundresses	Farmers, planters and overseers	Laundry work (hand)	Dressmakers and seamstresses	Other clerks (except clerks in	Saleswomen	Saleswomen (not elsewhere	Teachers (elementary school)	Teachers (elementary school)	Typists

6	Cotton-mill operators	Laun-dresses	Cotton-mill operators	Farmers and planters	Farm laborers (working out)	Laun-dresses (not in laundry)	Farm laborers (unpaid family workers)	Operators and kindred workers, apparel and accessories	Waitresses	Book-keepers	Waitresses
7	Laun-dresses	Seam-stresses	Farmers and planters	Cooks	Farm and plantation laborers	Sales-women (stores)	Book-keepers and cashiers	Book-keepers	Book-keepers	Waitresses	Sewers and stitchers
8	Woolen mill operators	Tailor-esses	Cotton mill operators	Sales-women	Stenog-raphers and typists	Book-keepers and cashiers	Laun-dresses (not in laundry)	Waitresses (except private family)	Sewers and stitchers, manufac-turing	Miscella-neous and not speci-fied operators	Nurses, registered
9	Farmers and planters	Woolen-mill operators	House-keepers and stewards	Farmers	Cooks	Trained nurses	House-keepers (private family)	Nurses, registered	Nurses, registered	Nurses, registered	Cashiers
10	Nurses	Hotel and restaurant employ-ees (not clerks)	Clerks and copyists	Seam-stresses	Sales-women (stores)	Farmers (general farms)	Other cooks	Trained nurses and stu-dent nurses	Tele-phone operators	Other service workers (except private house-hold)	Private household cleaners and servants

Note: Categories are given in order of size, and according to each census, regardless of changes in definition.

Sources: Decennial Census, 1870–1940; Janet M. Hooks, *Women's Occupations Through Seven Decades* (Women's Bureau Bulletin #218, U.S. Department of Labor); U.S. Dept. of Commerce, Bureau of the Census: Census of Population, 1960, Detailed Characteristics, U.S. Summary, Table 202; U.S. Department of Commerce, Bureau of the Census: Census of Population, 1970, Detailed Characteristics, U.S. Summary, PC (1) D1; U.S. Women's Bureau, "Occupations of Women, 1950, 1960, and 1970." Tables reprinted from the Economic Report of the President, 1973.

TABLE 1-4
Women's Labor Force Participation by Occupational Sector

Major Occupational Group	Percentage of all Working Women in this Field	Percentage of Workers in the Field who are Women	Women's Median Annual Salary (1977)	Women's Pay as a Percentage of Men's (1977)
Clerical	34.6	79.64	$ 8,601	61.9
Service	20.7	62.58	6,108	59.1
Professional and technical	15.6	42.70	11,995	65.8
Operative	11.8	31.76	7,350	58.3
Sales	6.9	44.80	6,825	42.5
Managerial and administrative	6.1	23.36	9,799	54.2
Craft and kindred	1.8	5.63	8,902	61.3
Farm	1.3	18.19	1,635	25.5

Source: 1978, *Employment and Training Report of the President,* 1979, Table A-16; *Earnings Gap,* U.S. Dept. of Commerce, Bureau of the Census, CPR P-60, #118.

earn only 59% of what men in the field are paid. This can occur because of outright discrimination, where women and men perform the same job but receive different pay, or because most of the women within a basic job sector are employed in the lower-paying jobs of that sector.

To illustrate the latter point, we can use the example of college teaching. As we would expect, the higher ranks of faculty are paid the most money—and they are predominantly male. Those in the lower ranks—instructors and lecturers—are more likely female and are paid less (see Table 1-5). But, you might argue, professors, be they male or female, *should* be paid more than instructors, since they are more qualified. Yet Table 1-5 shows that for every rank of teaching, men are paid more than women of the same rank. In addition, as shown in Table 1-6, female doctorates earn less than male doctorates in all fields, at various stages of their respective careers. And, contrary to what most people assume, the male–female earnings gap has been expanding over time, as can be seen in Figure 1-5.

These earnings figures are averages for male and female workers. If we examine the earnings data for non-white women, we see that their situation is even worse. Table 1-2 summarized the median earnings of different groups of minority women: white women, on the average, earn significantly more than all other groups of women, even

TABLE 1-5
Median Annual Salaries of Faculty in Colleges and Universities by Sex: 1973–1974

Faculty Rank	Median Salary Women	Median Salary Men	Percentage of Faculty who are Women	Women's Salary as a Percentage of Men's
Professor	$18,211	$19,932	8.9	91
Associate professor	14,634	15,376	15.2	95
Assistant professor	12,087	12,758	24.1	95
Instructor	9,700	10,212	44.8	95
Lecturer	12,670	13,254	38.5	96

Source: National Education Association (unpublished data).

though some of the other groups have a higher proportion of high school graduates and a higher level of average educational attainment. Thus minority women suffer double discrimination—as women and as members of a minority group.

Table 1-6
Median Annual Salaries of Full-Time Employed Doctorates by Sex and Years of Experience: 1979

Field of Doctorate	All Females	All Males	2–5 Years of Experience, Female	2–5 years of Experience, Male	6–10 Years of Experience, Female	6–10 Years of Experience, Male
All fields	$23,100	$30,000	$19,700	$22,300	$22,000	$26,000
Math	22,100	26,600	19,800	19,900	20,600	23,600
Computer sciences	25,200	28,500	—	22,300	24,600	28,300
Chemistry	24,300	31,300	22,200	24,600	22,700	27,800
Engineering	26,200	32,700	24,600	26,400	25,600	30,000
Medicine	25,600	32,800	23,100	24,500	23,300	29,200
Biology	22,400	28,200	18,300	20,500	21,100	24,700
Psychology	22,900	28,000	19,700	20,300	22,500	24,000
Social sciences	22,900	27,400	19,500	19,900	21,300	24,000

Source: National Research Council, Science, Engineering, and Humanities Doctorates in the United States, 1979 Profile, p. 21.

FIGURE 1-5
Median Earnings of Full-Time Workers,
14 Years of Age and Over, by Sex, 1957–1977

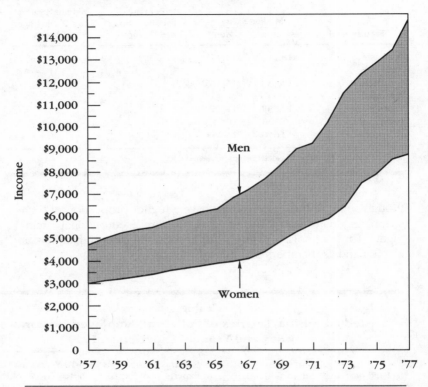

Source: U.S. Department of Commerce, Bureau of the Census.

Researchers have tried to analyze the differing occupational distributions of women of different ethnic groups to see if they match the pattern for white females more closely than the pattern for males of the same ethnic group. These researchers construct "indexes of occupational dissimilarity," which show the amount of hypothetical job changing that would be required for minority women to match, statistically, the white female reference group *or* their minority male reference group. Their conclusion was: "The occupational distributions of minority women are more like the distribution of white women than those of their minority male counterparts."[7] Thus gender, according to their findings, is a powerful determinant of labor market status for white *and* minority women. In later chapters we will explore the various theories that try to explain women's occupational distribution and lower wages. At this point, we are only trying to draw a clear picture of the position of working women in the labor force.

Unemployed Women

This picture, however, is still incomplete. Economists include in the labor force those who are employed, of course, and those who are looking for but haven't found work—the unemployed. The statistics on women's unemployment are quite bleak. As the data in Table 1-7 show, female unemployment rates have been consistently higher than male rates, and when male rates jump up, as in 1975, female rates go even higher. Looking at the third column of Table 1-7, we see more evidence of double discrimination: black women's unemployment rates are even higher, reaching 13.9% in June 1980.[8]

Why are women's unemployment rates higher than men's? Again, the popular myth that men are the real workers (women are not "by nature" in the labor force) may lead many employers to hire the male job seeker more readily than the female job seeker. Furthermore, some women are victims of the "last hired, first fired" rule, which

TABLE 1-7
Adult Unemployment Rates by Sex:
16 Years of Age and Older

	Male Unemployment Rate (Percent)	Female Unemployment Rate (Percent)	Black Female Unemployment Rate (Percent)
1949	5.9	6.0	7.9
1950	5.1	5.7	8.4
1955	4.2	4.9	8.4
1960	5.4	5.9	9.4
1965	4.0	5.5	9.2
1970	4.4	5.9	9.3
1975	7.9	9.2	14.0
1978	5.2	7.2	13.1

Source: Employment and Training Report of the President, 1979, Tables A-20 and A-21.

hits women who have recently entered nontraditional fields. Similarly, cuts in public sector employment may affect women severely, since large numbers of women are employed by state and local governments. Above all, during most economic downturns the myth that women do not "need" to work is usually revived as a justification for laying off women first.

Jobless But Not Counted: The Discouraged Workers

Women's high unemployment rates are only part of the problem of joblessness. The Department of Labor identifies another category of workers who exist in the penumbra of the labor force, the so-called *discouraged workers*. These are defined as workers who are out of work and who are not actively looking for a job anymore, so they have technically left the labor force. They are *not counted* as unemployed; indeed, if they were, the official unemployment rates would look much more threatening than they already do. Most labor economists will admit that frequently a drop in the official unemployment rate is only masking a large rise in the number of discouraged workers.

For example, from May 1980 to June 1980, the female unemployment rate dropped from 7.8% to 7.5%. Good news? Not exactly. The unemployment rate is derived from a proportion: the number of unemployed people (the numerator) divided by the number of people in the labor force (the denominator). Therefore, a decline in the unemployment rate *could* indicate that there are fewer unsatisfied job seekers (a decline in the numerator, with the denominator remaining the same or increasing), a happy circumstance. Alternatively, a decline could mean that a number of unsuccessful job seekers became discouraged and stopped looking for jobs, thereby lowering the numerator and the denominator of the proportion. In this case, a decline in the unemployment rate indicates an unhealthy economy, where workers have given up even looking for jobs. Which was it in June 1980, when unemployment fell? If we look at the data on the total size of the female labor force from May 1980 to June 1980, we find that it shrank from 44,663,000 to 44,416,000.[9] This gives us reason to suspect that the fall in the female unemployment rate merely masked a rise in the number of female discouraged workers.

In effect, the discouraged worker, fired or laid off, may realize that unemployment is so bad in her trade or region that it makes no sense even to go out and look for another job. Perhaps this became the fate of many women workers hired in the 1970s affirmative action upswing of the economy. During the 1980s recession, disproportionate numbers of women and blacks were fired or laid off, with the Justice Department aiding their exit from the labor force by loosening affirmative action standards. Indeed, about three times as many women as men are discouraged workers.[10] While many of these women cite their "home responsibilities" as the major obstacle keeping them from looking for a job, many others simply state that they do not think they can get a job, that no jobs are available. If we add these millions of female discouraged workers to the millions of unemployed women workers *in* the labor force, and these to the masses of underpaid employed women workers, we begin to get a picture of women's employment situation in America today.

More Uncounted Workers: The Subterranean Economy

This is only the beginning of the picture because it covers only legal, paid employment. As some economists are beginning to realize, in addition to such employment there is a large "subterranean economy" that escapes the GNP counters and, more importantly, the Internal Revenue Service. This subterranean economy includes illegal economic activity as well as work that *would* be legal if it were reported to the government for tax purposes. Although we do not have employment statistics for this sector, we do have some rough estimates of the volume of economic activity taking place. According to 1980 figures, the total value of economic activity in the U.S. subterranean economy was around $700 billion per year, or about 27% of the GNP.[11]

Within this subterranean economy we find a great deal of traditional women's work: undeclared work in a family business, babysitting and child care, small cottage industries or crafts for private sale or barter, "off-the-books" work in local businesses, and service-sector jobs where pay is mostly in unreported tips (such as in waitressing). Furthermore, many poor women are trying to support families with the aid of transfer payments (welfare), which they would lose if they reported their legal earnings; these women have a great incentive to stay "off the books." Other women who work in the subterranean economy are those who work in illegal occupations such as prostitution, drugs, and gambling. If economists were to analyze the subterranean economy in more detail, they might find that women workers outnumber male workers. It is unlikely that such detailed research will ever be carried out. But we should be aware that changes may be taking place in sectors excluded from the GNP.

Women's Unpaid Work

So far, we have looked only at women's waged labor. But women's productive work is not limited to waged labor. The real work that women do in housework, childbearing, and child rearing is all economically productive and vital to the economy, even if it is wageless work. While some married women may feel they receive a part of their husband's wages as their "pay" for their housework, this implicit wage may evaporate in the face of contested expenditures or divorce. In these cases, the power over the wage may return to its source, the husband. We shall examine the nature of this work in more detail later; for the present our discussion will be limited to estimating the extent of this unpaid labor. All the planning, shopping, cooking, and cleaning that must be done in every household if workers are to arrive at their jobs rested, fed, and ready to work is done almost exclusively by women. Depending on the number of children in the home and the woman's employment status, housework can absorb up to 10½ hours of the day, more than most full-time jobs! Even life insurance companies have begun to realize the value of the housewife's work. They warn policyholders that the "homemaker's" value, if she had to be replaced, comes to over $15,000 per year. In addition to housework, women's work in childbearing and child raising is unpaid, yet necessary and highly productive, since without this work there would be *no* labor force for the future. Women can spend from nine months to many years on this work (and rather than receive a wage for it, actually absorb large personal costs).

These last regions of women's economically productive work provide prime examples of the veil covering the woman worker. That housework and childbearing are real work, even if unpaid, is obvious when one examines the nature of the tasks involved or the importance of the work to the smooth functioning of the economy. Yet these jobs are rarely called work. They are usually considered as part of the woman's *role,* part of her "responsibilities," which should be performed even if she holds a full-time job outside of the home. In fact, in most households, when a woman decides to take paid employment, it is her responsibility to hire the "substitute" housekeeper, since housework is seen as her responsibility. Childbearing, similarly, is seen as an outgrowth of the "maternal instinct" and thus in the realm of emotions; it is not viewed as labor or work.

The veil covers women's paid labor as well. Labor market analysts have always emphasized that women's paid employment is simply an extension of women's traditional roles: the secretary is sometimes called an "office wife," the school teacher is seen as an extended mother, and the nurse is the nurturing healer. By categorizing women's participation in the labor force in this way, as an extension of women's nature and roles, the popular ideology of the woman worker as different from the male worker can be reinforced. Male workers are seen as the "real workers," since they work for the money; women workers are just extending their nurturing role, and the money is secondary. With this ideology—that women work out of love and not for the money—women's unpaid work in the home and women's paid work in the labor force is marginalized. And it is precisely this ideology that hides women's real economic oppression. Working for no pay in the household, underpaid in the labor force, and, as the bulk of the "discouraged workers," not even counted as unemployed since a woman's real *need* for paid employment is hardly recognized, women are put outside the cash-nexus economy.

Like everyone else, however, women need to work in order to eat. Women perform productive labor in the household, in the paid labor force, and in the subterranean economy, in spite of the mythology that women do not really work like men do. Having established women's real presence in the economy, we can now try to examine the development of women's work historically.

Additional Readings

C. Bell, "Women's Work: An Economic Appraisal"; F. Blau, "The Data on Women Workers, Past, Present and Future"; and E. Almquist and J. Wehrle-Einhorn, "The Doubly Disadvantaged: Minority Women in the Labor Force," *in* A. Stromberg and S. Harkess, *Women Working* (Mayfield Publishing Co., 1978).

K. Newland, *Women, Men, and the Division of Labor,* Worldwatch pamphlet #37.

The best sourcebook of economic statistics for American women, though somewhat dated, is the *1975 Handbook on Women Workers,* U.S. Department of Labor, Women's Bureau Bulletin #297, 1975.

Notes

1. L. Gurtin, "The Benefits of Family Stability," *Collegiate Forum,* Fall 1980, p. 12.
2. *Ibid.*

3. U.S. Department of Labor, Bureau of Labor Statistics, *Employment in Perspective: Working Women,* Report 611, July 1980 (hereafter referred to as *BLS 611*).

4. *Ibid.*

5. *Ibid;* first quarter of 1979 compared to first quarter of 1980.

6. *Ibid.*

7. E. Almquist and J. Wehrle-Einhorn, "The Doubly Disadvantaged: Minority Women in the Labor Force," *in* A. Stromberg and S. Harkess, *Women Working,* p. 80.

8. *BLS 611.*

9. *Ibid.*

10. *1975 Handbook on Women Workers* (Women's Bureau), p. 79.

11. See "Underground Economy Grows and Grows," *Wall Street Journal,* 10/20/80, which summarizes recent studies by the Atlanta Federal Reserve and by E. Feige of the University of Wisconsin.

Women's Work in America: From the Mayflower to the First Factories

After reading the description of the current state of women's work in the first chapter, there may be a temptation to reply, "This is nothing new; women have always been the breeders, feeders, and earners." But then you wonder if it *has* always been so. According to the romantics, after all, before the industrial revolution there were no factories and *everyone* worked in the home or on the family farm, women and men alike. Did the industrial revolution in America change women's work? Was it responsible for taking women out of the homes and putting them into factories? Or did it take men off the farms and put them into industry? To address these questions, we need to understand the dynamics of colonization and development in the United States before the industrial revolution.

Women's Work in the American Colonies

As most people remember from their history books, America was settled by land-hungry religious refugees and representatives of European trading companies interested in extracting valuable raw materials for export. With limited legal rights to own property, most women lacked this particular pecuniary incentive to weather the harsh Atlantic crossing and settle here. The desire for religious or political freedom, the desire for adventure, or the need to accompany their husbands brought some women to the American colonies. Other women had no choice: they were brought as slaves. Still others, serving prison terms in Europe, saw "transportation to the colonies" as the lesser of evils; it was more appealing than execution or life in an English jail. Transported criminals and debtors came to America as indentured servants, which meant working for a stipulated period of service until their debts were paid.

Altogether, relatively few women actually came to the New World. This shortage of women in the American colonies was lamented by the male settlers and by the trading companies alike. The companies knew their men would not stay in the New World very long without "family life." The Virginia Company, a major trading company, made this point explicitly:

> *That a fitt hundreth might be sent of woemen, maids young and uncorrupt to make wives to the inhabitants and by that means to make the men there more settled and lesse moveable who by defect thereof (as is credibly reported) stay there but to get something and then to return to for England, wch will breed a dissolucon, and so an overthrow of the Plantacon. These women if they marry to the public ffarmers, to be transported at the charges of the company; if otherwise, then those that takes them to wife to pay the said company their charges of transportation, and it was never fitter time to send them than nowe.*[1]

Without wives, the men would never stay in America; they would make their money and return to England. But if women could be imported to the colonies, then the men might marry and settle down, and business would prosper. Who should pay the passage for the women? The company would pay if the women married company men; if not, the husband-to-be would pay.

Occasionally, these schemes to import women backfired. The Company of the Indies, for example, sent a shipload of ex-prostitutes and other women from French jails to marry some French colonists. When these women arrived, they showed little inclination toward marriage or motherhood. After that fiasco, the company commissioned the Ursuline sisters to oversee their wife-importation schemes.[2] There are indications that some women were forcibly brought; abductors " '. . . took up rich yeoman's daughters to serve his Majesty as breeders in Virginia unless they paid money for their release. . . .' "[3] The majority of female-importation schemes, however, seem to have been fairly legitimate.

In addition to these direct importation schemes, women were offered various incentives to come and live in the female-scarce, labor-scarce colonies. In some colonies, they were given the right to own land or were *given* land under the "head-right" system. They could open their own businesses and enter most trades, largely unencumbered by English common law or guild restrictions. Since the deficit of females was not only an obstacle to establishing stable colonies, but also meant a permanent labor shortage in New World settlements, pronatal policies were enacted as well.

There are several ways labor-scarce societies can encourage the necessary population increase. They can promote earlier marriages, more births per marriage, easy divorces with quick remarriages, and short mourning periods with quick remarriages. In addition, they can try to reduce infant mortality, and they can ban abortions and/or infanticides, and look leniently at unwed mothers. Given the range of customs in the different colonies, evidence can be found for *all* of these policies. While this will not suffice to prove that these particular policies had pronatal results, certain perspectives on the various colonial policies can be gained.

When a society encourages early marriages, the childbearing time span is usually lengthened, which should have pronatal results. Colonial women may have appeared to have married earlier than their English sisters, especially if we believe this report from North Carolina in the 1730s:

> *They marry generally very young, some at thirteen or fourteen, and she that continues unmarried until twenty is reckoned a stale maid.... A colonial spinster of over twenty-five was regarded as a hopeless and confirmed old maid.*[4]

Since modern historians have found that colonial women usually married in their twenties, at least in the North, it is likely that contemporary observers were impressed with the relative *ease* of marriage in the New World and the apparent liberality of our courtship customs, such as unchaperoned dating and bundling.[5]

Many colonies offered financial incentives to marry. Some towns gave building lots as wedding presents to young couples; others imposed taxes on bachelors and limited their freedoms. Sometimes the penalty for not marrying was severe. For example, early Maryland laws forced women to marry within seven years of inheriting property:

> *That it may be prevented that no woman here vow chastity in the world, unless she marry within seven years after land fall to her, she must either dispose away of her land ... it is gonne unless she git a husband.*[6]

Of course, early marriage *alone* cannot guarantee children. Ideally, the partners should also be compatible. While laws can never guarantee happy (and thus fecund) marriages, they can permit fast dissolution of unhappy marriages. Contrary to our images of Puritan family life, divorces, for example, were relatively easy to obtain. Grounds for divorce in the American colonies included more than the standard adultery or desertion claims, the courts lending a sympathetic ear to charges of mental or physical abuse, other forms of cruelty, or stinginess. Liberalized divorce, in the context of a social compulsion to remarry, can result in higher proportions of happy marriages with greater numbers of children. Toward this end, quick remarriage of spouses after death or divorce was an established custom in the colonies. Widowers remarried so swiftly that it was not considered tasteless to serve the leftovers from the funeral wake at the wedding feast![7] So intense was the pronatal climate of the colonies that unwed mothers were tolerated as well. As a French observer explained:

Citizens are so precious in the new country that a girl, by rearing her child, seems to atone for the initial sin. . . .[8]

Colonial women seem to have remarried frequently and to have given birth to numerous children, even if many never lived to adulthood. While the average number of surviving children per family was probably seven or eight, many women were famous for their prodigious fertility. Note, for example, this 1751 eulogy for a colonial wife:

Also she was a fruitful vine
the truth I may relate—
Fourteen was of her body born
and lived to mans estate.
From these did spring a numerous race,
one hundred thirty-two;
Sixty and six each sex alike
As I declare to you.
And one thing more remarkable
which I shall here record,
She'd fourteen children with her
At the table of our Lord.[9]

Given the labor-scarce situation in the colonies then, women's childbearing work was actively encouraged. Yet these colonial women worked hard in their homes as well, producing goods for the family's use or for barter or sale to others. Most goods used in the home were produced by the wife under quite primitive circumstances. Consider the preparation of food, for instance. Building the fire in the hearth was a painstaking chore using flint and steel. The pots and kettles were large and often made of iron, making them difficult to lift and carry. Meals themselves were composed of many elaborate courses, and everything was "made from scratch," which usually included such chores as slaughtering and dressing the pig or threshing the corn. Beyond cooking, the colonial wife's housework included regular polishing of the pewter, scrubbing the floor, ironing the linen, and so on. Ironically, it was probably the less fortunate women who had to work the fields all day, as this Maryland man reported in 1656:

The Women are not (as is reported) put into the ground to worke, but occupie such domestique imployments and housewifery as in England, that is dressing victuals, righting up the house, milking, imployed about dayries, washing, sowing, etc., and both men and women have times of recreations, as much or more than in any part of the world besides, yet some wenches that are nasty, beastly and not fit to be so imployed are put into the ground, for reason tells us, they must not at charge be transported, and then maintained for nothing.[10]

In the southern colonies wealthy women lived a remarkably different existence from that of poor, indentured, and slave women. White women of the slave-owning class were economically productive as childbearers and as household managers, but unlike their northern sisters, they were not supposed to be "earners," that is, to produce goods also. In fact, de-emphasis of their productive usefulness underlined their value to their husbands as "status items"; their ostensible idleness could be seen as a luxury good only the rich could afford.

Slave women were used for all three female productive capacities: childbearing, household work, and direct production of goods. But as slaves, all they produced was appropriated by the slave owner. The children they bore were *his* property, their housework (such as it was) maintained the labor power of *his* slave labor force, and the crops and other goods they produced were *his* property as well. The slave owners carefully evaluated the productivity of slave women in their various functions and usually allocated the women to different tasks so as to maximize productivity. Rarely has the value of women's labor in its different uses been calculated so carefully and so cruelly.

Later, during the Revolutionary period, women's productive work continued to play an important role in the survival of the nation. As Martha Washington so aptly said:

> *Whilst our husbands and brothers are examples of patriotism, we must be patterns of industry.*[11]

During the Revolution, some women maintained production on the family farms, others dressed as men and fought, and some worked as "camp followers"—the squadrons of women who traveled with the troops, preparing food, shelter, and clothing for the soldiers. Not all women were swept away with patriotism, however. The first sit-down strike in America was by washerwomen in Virginia who refused to launder uniforms for the pittance they were offered.[12] After the Revolution, women organized boycotts and demonstrations again (the earlier Boston "tea party" protested British price hikes) to protest high food prices and shortages.

Amid the economic turmoil of the post-Revolution period, we find the first real evidence of interest in the use of women's labor outside the home sphere. In 1789, for instance, there was a petition in favor of a cotton factory stating that, " 'it will afford employment to a great number of women and children, many of whom will be otherwise unless if not burdensome to society.' " A year earlier a factory in Boston had received public approval because it promised 'to give employment to a great number of persons, especially females, who now eat the bread of idleness.' "[13] American industrial interests did not become fully active, however, until after the War of 1812, when they opened battle against the agricultural interests over tariff protection for infant industries.

Women and the First Industrial Revolution: 1814 to the Civil War

To understand the pivotal role of female labor in the industrialization of America, it is necessary to examine the economic policy debates of the Hamiltonians and Jeffersonians in the early 1800s. Essentially, the Hamiltonian industrial interests pressed for tariffs on imports to protect infant industry in America. The Jeffersonian agricultural interests were opposed to fostering industry in America, claiming it would divert labor from the soil to the cities, as it had in England. The industrial interests prevailed. They based their argument on the use of female labor. Women, supposedly inessential for agriculture, could form the labor force for industry in America. As Hamilton himself argued:

> *Women and children are rendered more useful than they otherwise would be.... The husbandman himself (would experience) a new source of profit and support from the increased activity of his wife and daughters invited and stimulated by the demands of the neighboring manufactories....*[14]

In other words, industry would not steal men away from agriculture, but would simply use women's labor more productively. Furthermore, in manufacturing, women would learn good, industrious habits, and their families would benefit from their earnings. And no one would have to fear that industrial work would spoil women's childbearing capacity or taste for marriage, since wage-earning women would

> *... become eligible partners for life for young men, to whom they will be able to afford substantial aid in the support of families. Thus the inducement to early marriages ... is greatly increased ... and immensely important effects produced on the welfare of society.*[15]

Since the labor scarcity had dictated higher wages here than in Europe, the agriculturalists had argued that Americans could never really compete with English industry. But again, the industrialists argued, the use of female labor in American factories would make the difference:

> *It has been alleged that wages were too high in America to admit of our entering into competition in manufactures with the older countries of Europe, particularly Britain. We believe the opinion is not well founded ... women and children who perform a great part of the work can be hired nearly as low here as in England.*[16]

Although the industrial interests prevailed, it was really the embargo on foreign imports during the War of 1812 that stimulated domestic factory production. Since these early factories were staffed almost exclusively by women, they will be described in some detail.

The first textile factories were water-powered; thus they were located near their power sources—that is, by rivers—and not in the urban areas, which would have afforded a local labor supply. To organize a labor force for these textile factories, the mill owners followed two basic patterns, either the Lowell or the Slater system.

At Lowell (and at Waltham and other towns), the textile company built the mill and then constructed boarding houses for the workers, usually farm girls recruited by company agents roaming the country-

TABLE 2-1
Wages in the Waltham Mills: 1821

Weekly Wages	Number of Women	Number of Men
Under $2.00	7	—
$2.00 to $2.49	129	3
$2.50 to $2.99	82	1
$3.00 to $3.49	58	5
$3.50 to $3.99	7	2
$4.00 or over	1	52
Total	284	63

Source: E. Abbott, *Women in Industry,* 1919, p. 278.

side. Why did the girls leave their farms to come to Lowell? One mill girl explained:

> *Indeed the most prevailing incentive was to secure the means of education for some* male *member of the family. To make a* gentleman *of a brother or a son, to give him a college education, was the dominant thought in the minds of a great many of these provident mill girls. . . .*[17]

Also, many girls saved their wages to generate a dowry for marriage. Certainly very few of them intended to spend their whole lives working in the mills.

Although the hours of work were long (up to 14 hours a day), the work intensity was not severe, at least in the early years of the Massachusetts mills. In fact, the girls generated a whirl of cultural activities around their work places, starting magazines (such as the *Lowell Offering*) and reading circles that became quite famous. Wages for these mill girls, which were reduced by the obligatory room and board charges, were lower than prevailing rates for male labor and even less than the rates for women in domestic service. The data in Table 2-1 on wages in the Waltham Mills reveal two important points: women formed the majority of the work force in the typical early factories, and male workers were clustered in the higher-paying ranks, usually as foremen.

Even if wages were relatively low, the mill girls felt they had more "culture" and independence than domestic work would have offered. Indeed, although they had originally been considered an ideal labor force, due to their cheapness, facility, and docility, these early mill workers soon taught the factory owners a few lessons. The mill girls did not actually unionize (which was of dubious legality anyway), but they formed "protective associations" and held "turnouts"—spontaneous factory walkouts.

Their ingenuity was remarkable. Describing an 1834 strike in Lowell over the threat of reduced wages, a contemporary wrote:

> *They held several meetings or caucuses, at which a young girl presided, who took an active part in persuading her associates to give notice that they should quit the mills and to induce them to "make a run" on the Lowell bank and the savings bank, which they did....* [18]

Not only did the Lowell banks have to send to Boston for gold, but this strike gathered some 800 to 2,000 women workers (the accounts vary), with additional others who threatened to quit work if the strikers' demands were not met.

The famous independence of the Lowell mill girls was undercut by the 1840s, when factory owners started using the growing immigrant labor supply to staff the mills. As working conditions deteriorated, many of the New England girls left the mills, unable to mount an effective resistance.

In fact, the paternalistic Lowell-type factory model proved to be a lot more cumbersome to manage than the factory system that had developed in Rhode Island, the Slater system. Slater's factories employed families of workers. The labor contract stipulated the family members who worked in the mill, their wage rates, and housing costs. Family wages were paid in credit at the company store, a notorious source of extra company profits. Unionization was limited in these factories as well: workers had to sign "yellow-dog" contracts, swearing not to organize, and employers blackballed troublemakers. Strikes by these workers meant not only the loss of wages, but also no food or housing, since the company owned everything.

In general, by the 1840s, women industrial workers in the cities, in the Lowell-type mills, and in the Slater-type mills were facing serious problems. Factory work conditions had eroded, because technological change had increased the speed and complexity of machinery. The increasing immigrant labor supply had eliminated any scarcity of labor, so workers could no longer resist working longer hours, especially as wage rates fell. Within the factories, the mystique of benevolent paternalism had given way to more modern management techniques; in the 1840s, Lowell overseers began to be paid bonuses for increasing the women's output.

Women Workers Outside the Factories

As factory conditions declined, the women's magazines began to promote a new ideology for women, the dream of home and hearth. Often termed the "cult of true womanhood," this early version of the feminine mystique stressed women's basic weaknesses and unfitness for factory labor. As a popular writer, Mrs. Sanford, wrote in 1842:

> *A really sensible woman feels her dependence. She does what she can, but she is conscious of inferiority, and therefore grateful for support.*[19]

Women's idleness became a new status symbol, the total reversal of an earlier Puritan caution that women's idle hands would make mischief. Correspondingly, the literature of the mid-1800s reveals a tension between women of different classes. Most likely, women recently "released" from the necessity to work, or women in professions trying to justify their existence in the labor force as genteel, socially acceptable types, felt somewhat threatened by working class women: these women were doing "men's" work and generally spoiling the image of delicate womanhood. Read, for example, this 1857 reply of a woman teacher to a newspaper series, "A Factory Girl":

> *I do claim to be superior to the vulgar herd with which our factories are stocked, and I do consider them unfit to associate with me, or to move in the same society to which I belong. Such, too, is the sentiment of all "Upper Tendom".* . . . [20]

Many women who left the factories did not retire to the hearth or develop genteel sensibilities. Instead, they joined the pioneer movements going West. Their reasons were varied. Some professed noble missionary zeal, others went to improve their failing health, and still others went simply to accompany their husbands, or to find husbands. Also, many went West just to make money (the original American gold diggers). The westward crossing involved so much work and so many casualties that pioneer women usually ended up doing both traditionally female work (cooking and washing) and traditionally male work (hunting, collecting dung, and so on). If they made it to the end, the women settlers were responsible for constructing a household and raising children, and they usually had a cash sideline as well, such as feeding boarders, selling eggs, or teaching school. As one pioneer woman wrote, in utter despair, "I hear hogs in my kitchen."[21]

Notes

1. A. Calhoun, *Social History of the American Family,* Vol. I, p. 216.

2. *Ibid*, p. 333.

3. *Ibid*, p. 217.

4. *Ibid*, p. 245.

5. Potter, *in* D. V. Glass and D. E. C. Eversley, eds., *Population in History,* p. 65n. Bundling was a system of premarital bedsharing. The fully clothed (bundled) houseguest would be bedded with a similarly dressed member of the host's household.

6. Calhoun, p. 247.

7. *Ibid*, p. 248.

8. *Ibid*, p. 89.

9. *Ibid*.

10. C. Holliday, *Woman's Life in Colonial Days,* p. 272.

11. *Ibid*, p. 136.

12. W. Blumenthal, *Women Camp Followers of the American Revolution,* p. 45, 46.

13. Quoted by E. Abbott, "The History of Industrial Employment of Women in the United States," *Journal of Political Economy* (1906), p. 492.

14. *Ibid,* p. 493.

15. *Ibid,* p. 498.

16. From the 1817 "Memorial on Manufactures from Citizens of Baltimore" quoted in Abbott, p. 498n.

17. C. Ware, *The Early New England Cotton Manufacture,* p. 218.

18. *Lowell Journal* account, quoted in Andrews and Bliss, *History of Women in Trade Unions in the United States,* p. 27.

19. B. Welter, "The Cult of True Womanhood," *American Quarterly* (1966), p. 159.

20. D. Walkowitz, "Working Class Women in the Gilded Age," *Journal of Social History* (1972), p. 469.

21. See the selection with this title in the excellent anthology, *Let Them Speak for Themselves: Women in the American West 1849–1900,* edited by C. Fischer.

3

Women's Work in Post-Civil War America

While some women abandoned their factory jobs to go West or to become "ladies," they were always replaced by new waves of immigrant workers. But the Civil War broke this rhythm. Lack of cotton shut down the textile factories. When men went to fight, it created new employment opportunities for women, particularly in clerical work, nursing, and war industries.

The peace at Appomattox was only the lull before a storm. America's second "industrial revolution"—fueled by new technological advances, new fortunes, and a supportive political climate—was under way. A transition to mass production, which began in the post-Civil War period, had profound implications for American workers and for women workers in particular. The technological advances that allowed full mechanization of production, culminating in the assembly-line factory, dramatically changed the work process by deskilling the various trades. Tasks formerly performed by skilled male workers could now be done by unskilled, lower-waged replacements. In the post-War period, there was no shortage of replacements: masses of immigrants, women, and emancipated blacks needed jobs. The only hold the skilled workers had on their jobs was their unions. Not that the union movement of the 1800s had been particularly powerful; rather, in the post-Civil War period, skilled tradesmen turned to their unions to secure job rights.

Women Workers and the Trade Unions

While employers were using their influence over the design and implementation of technological change to threaten skilled laborers, workers turned to the trade union movement in defense. The unions' defense of the threatened workers, however, could be considered nostalgic at best. Under the leadership of Samuel Gompers, the trade union movement stubbornly adhered to a rather anachronistic, almost pastoral fantasy: if all wives left the labor force and returned to hearth and home, their husbands would have all the jobs. With less competition for jobs, wages would increase, and everyone would be better off than before. The union members agreed that all they needed was exclusive job access, by union or closed-shop agreements, for their dream to come true. Then all they would need was to keep women (and blacks and Orientals) out of their unions, and these groups would be out of the labor market as well.

This scenario, however, never took place. The unions could not win that essential job control battle; in the strikes of the late nineteenth century they were no match against the armed forces of their employers. The union strategy backfired, since employers found they could break strikes by replacing the skilled men with those very women the unions had excluded.

Thus the policies of the male-led trade union movement shaped women's participation in the industrial labor force during the post-Civil War period. Furthermore, these union constraints largely determined even the peculiar structure of the women's union movement. It is essential, then, to examine the policies of the major male trade unions in some detail. How, exactly, did they justify exclusion of women from membership? What did they do when women workers broke their strikes? Why did some unions let women join, on a "cut-rate dues, cut-rate benefits" basis? Were any unions genuinely sympathetic toward women? How did women workers respond? With these questions in mind, we shall explore the post-Civil War unionization experience.

At the national level, the major union organizations after the Civil War were the Knights of Labor (1869) and the American Federation of Labor (1886). By 1880 women were admitted to the Knights under the organization's national policy; however, their female investigator found that many locals did not allow women. In addition, the principle of equal pay was found to be nothing but a "mockery."[1]

The American Federation of Labor's Positions on Women Workers

In the late 1880s the Knights were already overshadowed by the growth of the American Federation of Labor (the AFL). A look at the AFL's official record on women is useful. In 1882 they allowed representation of women's labor organizations, in 1883 they approved of equal pay, and in 1885 they urged the organization of working women. By 1890 the first official female delegate came to their convention. But in 1892 and 1894 they urged special legislation for women only. They endorsed the eight-hour workday for women and the prohibition of female employment on foot-powered machinery. In 1898 they introduced a resolution at their national convention to ask the U.S. Congress

> *to remove all women from government employment, and thereby to encourage their removal from the "everyday walks of life and relegate them to the home."*[2]

The leading figure in the AFL's anti-women worker campaign was none other than their president, Samuel Gompers. His remarks in 1887

> *We know to our regret that too often are wives, sisters and children brought into the factories and workshops only to reduce the wages and displace the labor of men—the heads of families.*[3]

only foreshadowed his 1906 position paper on working women, which is worthwhile quoting at length:

> *I contend that the wife or mother, attending to the duties of the home, makes the greatest contribution to the support of the family . . . I entertain no doubt but that from the constant better opportunity resultant from the larger earning power of the husband the wife will, apart from performing her natural household duties, perform that work which is most pleasureable for her, contributing to the beautifying of her home and surroundings. In our time, and at least in our country generally speaking, there is no necessity for the wife contributing to the support of the family by working— that is . . . by wage labor. In our country . . . producing wealth in such prodigious proportions the wife as a wage-earner is a disadvantage economically considered, and socially is unnecessary.*[4]

TABLE 3-1
Women's Labor Force Participation in Various Industrial Sectors

Sector	1860	1890
Textiles	53.4%	40.6%
Clothing	45.0%	55.9%
Tobacco and cigars	13.9%	37.5%
Paper and printing	27.3%	24.8%

Note: Percentages given represent the proportion of women to all workers in each sector.
Source: Kuczynski (p. 76) from Senate Hearings, 1910.

Gompers conveniently forgot that most working class families in America still needed the woman's earnings in order to survive, especially when the husband's wages were low or nonexistent.

Gompers' statements were not pure rhetoric. They represented a significant endorsement of the strategies followed by some major AFL unions to preserve their privileged trades against the encroachments of women, blacks, immigrants, and unskilled workers of all descriptions. Which trades were these? An inspection of the sectoral distribution of women industrial workers (Table 3-1) reveals the major sectors where women formed a large proportion of the labor force. It is in these sectors that women's struggles with organized labor were the most difficult, since by their numbers women were a realistic alternative to a male work force (and a difficult mass to assimilate into a male-dominated union). In other words, unions in these sectors felt the threat of replacement by women much more directly than did unions in trades with few women. The resistance of these male cigar makers, printers, textile workers, and others often took rather subtle forms.

Cigar making, for instance, was originally done by women in their homes. It was only with increased popularity and demand for cigars that it became a male-dominated (skilled) trade, although women still did subsidiary aspects of the work. With large-scale immigration of Bohemian cigar makers to the United States in the 1860s, and with technological change enabling the use of molds for cigar-forming (formerly the major skilled aspect of the trade), women were again used in all aspects of cigar making, and it became a basic tenement industry.

The share of women as a percentage of employees in this field went from 9% in 1860, to 17% in 1880, and to 37% in 1900.[5] Male cigar makers watched this threat and reacted. In 1865 the Cigar Makers International union established male-only membership. A year later they debated on whether to allow women to work in union shops. But in 1869, employers used women to break a cigar-makers strike in New York City, and women replaced men striking against molding machines in 1870. Thus it was obvious that women were capable replacements for striking male cigar makers, and accordingly, in 1875, the national union decided to end their policy of barring women.

However, not all union members adhered to the new policy. Cincinnati cigar makers, for example, objected to the national union's looser stand on women in the trade and struck to remove women from their shops. The Cincinnati newspaper's comment on their action was direct: " 'The men say the women are killing the industry. It would seem that they hope to retaliate by killing the women.' "[6] By 1878, however the president of the national union conceded:

> *This state of affairs cannot be altered, it is better to unite than strike against them, because the latter course would prove futile, the employment of women having increased in alarming proportion.*[7]

But just one year later the cigar makers had developed a new strategy to fight women in the factories:

> *We cannot drive the females out of the trades but we can restrict this daily quota of labor through factory laws. No girl under eighteen should be employed more than eight hours per day; all overwork should be prohibited; white married women should be kept out of the factories at least six weeks before and six weeks after confinement.*[8]

Out of necessity, the cigar makers would admit women to membership. But to restrict women's competition in the trade, the union would push for "protective legislation." Where direct exclusion had failed, the indirect route might succeed.

The history of labor in the printing trades provides a similar story. Women were as good as men at most tasks of the trade, and mechanization threatened the skilled male workers' control over the better jobs. The traditional policy of the printing unions was to exclude women; in 1854 the national union made its opposition to women compositors explicit. But women were employed as printers, at lower wages, in spite of union opposition. Eventually, the national union agreed to allow women to form separate locals, which they did in various cities in 1868. Bitter infighting surrounded this policy, as is evident from the women's report to the national union (ITU) in 1871:

> *We refuse to take the men's situations when they are on "strike"; and when there is no strike, if we ask for work in union offices we are told there are no conveniences for us. We are ostracized in many offices because we are members of the union, and although the principle is right, the disadvantages are so many that we cannot much longer hold together....*[9]

By 1872, the national convention recommended that the women's locals be integrated with the men's, in order to enforce their equal pay policy. The intent was clear: with integrated locals, male printers could ensure that female printers weren't undercutting the pay scale. Since few employers would hire female printers when they could hire males at the same wage, this "equal pay" policy would drive women out. This interpretation of their integration and equal pay policies might appear somewhat paranoic, since women usually *wanted* equal treatment. But contrast their policies toward women with their policies toward older journeymen in the trade and their intentions become more obvious. The union allowed older journeymen, perhaps seen as less efficient by employers, to work for lower wage scales so as to overcome employer prejudice. To insist on "the rate for the job" for women and to tolerate lower pay scales for the older workers indicates the union's underlying objectives: equal treatment of women would result in unequal opportunity to work.

Wage scales were not the only means by which the union fought its women. With the introduction of lighter machinery, it became possible for women to enter more phases of the production process. For instance, when, in 1887, the linotype was introduced, the comment was made that women could run this machine quite easily. The unions' response? They required full training in all phases of printing—a four-year apprenticeship—before a union worker could operate the linotype. By continually requiring this apprenticeship in all aspects of the trade for jobs that did not require these capabilities at all, the unions could exclude women who could not afford a long period of apprenticeship. As a result of these tactics, women turned to the non-union shops. An 1889 survey of publishing houses in San Francisco, for example, found that the union shops were less than 3% female, while the non-union shops were over 50% female.[10]

Many AFL unions excluded women totally, and others admitted women only to keep them from effective competition for jobs. The tactics varied, even if the basic objective did not. As women realized that the male trade union movement, as led by the AFL, was not interested in their problems, they tried a different approach. They formed a women's union movement, the National Women's Trade Union League (NWTUL); it was founded in 1903 during an AFL national convention.

The National Women's Trade Union League

The NWTUL platform endorsed equal pay for equal work, organization of all workers into unions, the eight-hour workday, minimum wage scales, and full citizenship rights for women. Conceived with a nervous and paternalistic blessing from Gompers, who was dubious about a union-organizing group with non-trade union members, the NWTUL was largely composed of "ally" members (women with sympathies for unions). It devoted its early energies to publicizing the plight of working girls to the public, particularly to rich women who could donate money. Essentially, AFL tolerated the NWTUL, as long as they raised their own funds to organize women and they did not challenge any AFL policies. The NWTUL's major problem was their ambiguous legitimacy; the AFL repeatedly ignored their requests for real recognition, such as their 1907 request for a female organizer.

Compounding the NWTUL's problem with the AFL were its internal difficulties. Although the organization was composed of women from very different classes, the theory was that "sisterhood is powerful," or at least more powerful than class distinctions. But upper class women had the leisure time to organize meetings and the rich friends who could subsidize strikes. Although these "allies" may have been charitable, their interests often strayed into uplift activities, away from the more class-conscious functions of unions. Together with sister organizations such as the National Consumer's League, they undertook research on the working conditions facing women in industry.

In the early 1900s, many unions, like the cigar-makers mentioned earlier, had accepted women for membership while arguing for legal restrictions on their hours of work in order to limit their competition. The NWTUL's uplift theme neatly dovetailed the AFL's policy here: "Save the poor working woman. She works 14 hours a day in the factory, then more hours at home; for such low wages she barely survives." Their solution? Urge the states to pass "protective legislation," which would forbid women to work night jobs, or more than eight hours per day, and so on. Whether working women could survive on the earnings of eight hours of labor or whether employers would want to hire them given the restrictions on their employment—these fundamental questions were ignored.

Protective Legislation: Shifting the Responsibility for Women Workers onto the State

Protective legislation for women was defined as being under the state's jurisdiction, which implies that a woman's labor is not solely of interest to the woman herself, but also to the law because of the social effects. The legality of passing maximum-hours laws was usually defined through interpretation of the state's policing powers under the Fourteenth Amendment. For example, in the case of epidemics, the state can pass certain laws to protect the public, even if these laws abridge some individual rights.

The legal argument ran as follows. First, women are physically weak:

> *That woman's physical structure and the performance of maternal functions place her at a disadvantage in the struggle for subsistence is obvious.*[11]

Her weakness, combined with work, will jeopardize her childbearing function, which is not in society's general interest:

> *... a long time on her feet at work, repeating this from day to day, tends to injurious effects upon the body, and as healthy mothers are essential to vigorous offspring, the physical well-being of woman becomes an object of public interest and care in order to preserve the strength and vigor of the race.*[12]

Even if individual women and men are not concerned about this deterioration of childbearing, the state must abridge her freedom of contract in its own interest:

> *... her physical structure and proper discharge of her maternal functions—having in view not merely her own health, but the well being of the race—justify legislation to protect her from the greed as well as the passion of man. The limitations which this statute*

places on her contractual powers, upon her right to agree with her employer as to the time she shall labor, are not imposed solely for her benefit, but also largely for the benefit of all.[13]

Since the individual woman worker might not find this "protection" in her interest, the state becomes the agency to protect "society's" interest. As a corollary to this argument, legal arguments often implied that women were unequal bargainers in the labor market and therefore needed protection from the immorality that might ensue from their relative helplessness.

Who supported protective legislation? There is little evidence of the reactions of rank-and-file women workers. Some told the labor department of the effects of legislation on their jobs:

Now, they said, they are under constant pressure from their supervisors to work harder; they are told the sales of their departments must increase to make up for the extra amount the firm must pay in wages....[14]

As we have seen, male trade unionists favored legislation that would limit women's competition. In fact, some rank-and-file men even decided that *they* would enjoy an eight-hour day. Gompers squashed the idea quickly, as he declared:

An 8-hour day established by law is enforced by government agents. The workers' welfare is taken from under their immediate control ... it has been demonstrated that when the achievement of economic ends is entrusted to governmental agents, economic organization is weakened. So proceeds the vicious circle that saps the strength and vitality of the only dependable protection for the toilers. Some trades have established the 8-hour day by legislation. The miners of Missouri did, and their organization has dwindled away and the spirit of progress has departed with it....[15]

Basically, the AFL thought that the trade union movement should fight for men's rights and that the state should look after women. While the NWTUL and other "social conscience" organizations promoted protective legislation, a few women's groups opposed "women only" legislation. As they put it:

Welfare legislation ... will protect women to the vanishing point.[16]

Although most states passed protective legislation, its short-term labor market impact was difficult to assess. There were enough exceptions written into the laws to satisfy most employers, and inspection for violations was rare. But its ideological impact was significant. Throughout the agitation for passage of legislation and the series of court battles testing its legality, a new ideology about the woman worker was constructed.

Protective Legislation Reconstructs the Image of Women Workers

What were these new, twentieth-century ideas about the woman worker? As mentioned earlier, she was considered weak, both physically and with respect to her bargaining power; she needed the state's protection. Trade unions protected men, the state protected women. Furthermore, physical labor could damage women's childbearing capability, which became an issue of national concern. There are implications in the legal arguments that women sometimes *enjoyed* their work (but in an unladylike fashion):

> *The moral aspect of the subject of the employment of Negro women in the furnace room is, on the whole, of much more importance than is the question of the effect of the work on health. . . . A large number (of women) seemed to regard it (profanity) jocosely or as a matter of course, a few boasting that they gave the men word for word every time they were cursed. . . .*[17]

Similarly, some women enjoyed the *income* from their work and thereby did not service their husbands and children adequately:

> *. . . numbers of married women apply for employment because with the chance to labor at night, they can make a very good weekly income. . . . There is a grave question in the minds of the employers . . . whether it is in the best interests of the factories themselves and the workers to grant this request of the married women. . . . There is no doubt that the employment of married women at night naturally entails some neglect of the household duties during the day . . . it is possible that the husband and father does not receive his proper share of attention. Very likely the children suffer also.*[18]

The twentieth-century ideology of women's work was a far cry from the early Puritan ethic, which was grounded in a labor-scarce situation. The more modern stereotype, based on a labor-surplus economy, defined the woman as a nonworker, incapable of full participation in the labor force and in need of protection from the state, since she could not achieve protection by uniting with other workers as the male trade unionists could. Furthermore, since the states used their interest in women's childbearing to justify passage of the protective laws, a woman's maternal functions were emphasized as her prime contribution and as her major defining feature.

While protective legislation wrote women out of the definition of the "real" labor force, it paved the way for some new definitions of "a woman's place." Having become a "national resource," women could be ushered into the labor force for national emergencies. During World Wars I and II, women were urged to contribute their labor to the war effort, as a specific instance of national service. War work was not to be viewed as a permanent arrangement, but merely as a temporary necessity. Women in the twentieth century were to be our high-quality industrial reserve—skilled, well disciplined, and always available.

The second major role for women in the post-protection era was to be organized consumers. By 1900 there was much discussion of how to make housewives *feel* more productive; there was even some talk of a "housewife wage." Accompanying this was the new "science" of home economics, which was actually seen as a progressive solution to the woman question:

> *Now the family is conservative because it is the natural unit not of production but of consumption, and consumption is not easily revolutionized. For the purpose of using its resources society is less effectively organized than for creating them, since it does not recognize the management of consumption as a validly accredited career.* [19]

It was felt that women should aid social progress by managing the consumption work of society. From a business perspective, an increasingly diversified product market made it useful to have a group of people devoted to studying the variety of commodities available, focusing on consumption. As a writer in the 1930s commented:

> *In times when every dollar takes on the aspect of a life preserver, the knowledge that women do 80% of the retail purchasing in this country is less casually dismissed.* [20]

Women's consumerism was supposed to be good for the nation, good for business, and good for women, too. It was considered a pacifying diversion for women:

> *The restless desire for a change in fashions is a healthy outlet.... And to those who cannot change their whole lives or occupations*

even a new line in a dress is often a relief. The woman who is tired of her husband, or her home or her job feels some lifting of the weight of life from seeing a straight line change into a bouffant or a gray pass into beige. . . .[21]

Even as the ideology defined childbearing, consumerism, and national emergency employment as women's productive roles in the twentieth century, women themselves still remained in the labor force. Both the need for work and the desire for work have remained compelling reasons for women's continued labor force participation in the modern period.

The ideology of protection seems only to have reinforced the difficulties working women faced. It left women isolated from the trade union movement. It pushed women out of the industrial sector of the economy, which was covered by legislation, into the service and clerical fields, reinforcing existing tendencies toward occupational segregation. And with all that protection by the state, women still barely earned a living wage. Couldn't the government have legislated higher wages for women, instead of shorter hours? Why are women's wages so low? The question of wages, a theme throughout this account of the history of women's work in America, will be examined in detail in the next chapter.

Additional Readings

Readers wishing to study the source material on the history of women's work in America have a choice between original historical works (many reprinted by Arno Press) and modern anthologies of selected materials. Edith Abbott's 1910 classic, *Women in Industry* (republished by Arno Press, 1969) is an excellent source, as are her many articles on women workers in the various trades. Carl Holliday's 1922 study, *Women's Life in Colonial Days* (republished by Unger, 1960) gives a very complete account of this rarely discussed period. John Andrews and W. P. D. Bliss's *History of Women in Trade Unions in the United States* (Vol. X, U.S. Congress Report on the Condition of Women and Child Wage Earners, Washington, D.C., 1911) may be very dry reading, but remains one of the few reliable surveys of women's trade union activities for this period. A brilliant antidote to the poor style of the government studies can be found in the works of Elizabeth Hawes. Her witty *Why Women Cry Or Wenches with Wrenches* (1943) is a firsthand account of the experience of war work by an American woman.

Two good anthologies of historical writings are W. E. Brownlee and Brownlee, eds., *Women in the American Economy: A Documen-*

tary History (Yale University Press, 1976) and Baxandall, Gordon and Reverby, eds., *America's Working Women* (Vintage, 1976).

Notes

1. T. Wolfson, *The Woman Worker and the Trade Unions,* p. 64.
2. G. Boone, *The WTUL in Great Britain and the United States,* p. 54.
3. S. Gompers, *Labor and the Employer,* p. 118.
4. *Ibid,* pp. 122, 123.
5. Data from E. Abbott, *Women in Industry,* p. 195.
6. *Ibid,* p. 207n., from *Cincinnati Daily Inquirer,* 1877.
7. Quoted in F. Wolfe, *Admission to American Trade Unions* (1912), p. 81, from *Cigar Makers' Official Journal,* May 10, 1878.
8. Quoted in G. Boone, *The WTUL in Great Britain and the United States,* p. 94. Confinement refers to pregnancy.
9. E. Baker, *Technology and Women's Work,* p. 43.
10. A. Meyer, ed., *Woman's Work in America,* p. 302.
11. Muller v. Oregon, quoted in L. Kanowitz, *Sex Roles in Law and Society,* p. 47.
12. *Ibid.*
13. *Ibid.*
14. E. Hutchinson, *Women's Wages,* p. 135.
15. Gompers, *Labor and the Employer,* p. 101.
16. E. Baker, *Protective Labor Legislation,* p. 190.
17. L. Brandeis and J. Goldmark, *The Case Against Nightwork for Women,* p. 225.
18. *Ibid,* pp. 251, 252.
19. U. Weatherly, "How Does the Access of Women to Industrial Occupations React on the Family?" *American Journal of Sociology* (1909), p. 751.
20. Barnard, *in* M. Beard, *America Through Women's Eyes.*
21. Woodward, *in* M. Beard, *America Through Women's Eyes.*

Labor Market Work: Participation Rates and Wages

Returning to our present-day economy, our first task should be explain why women earn less than men, which would seem to be a question for the economists. The first economic model we will examine is an attempt to explain why people *enter* the labor market, that is, what determines their labor force participation rates. Once we have looked at this general model of labor force participation, we will see how it is modified to explain women's labor supply. Next we will move into the question of wages. The focus will be on the underlying assumptions and actual predictions of the various economists' models of wage discrimination, in order to evaluate the usefulness of the models. In the end, you will see that we may have to find other explanations for women's low wages.

What Determines Labor Force Participation?

For a long time economists have assumed that everyone decides whether to work and how much to work based on the value of their paycheck relative to the value of their leisure time. They figured that if your market wage rose, you would increasingly prefer the larger paycheck to your leisure time, within certain limits. Or, as they stated more formally, as wage rates increase, labor force participation rates should also increase. This simple labor–leisure choice is the basis, in fact, of the conventional upward-sloping supply-of-labor curve (refer to Figure 4-1).

FIGURE 4-1
The Labor-Supply Curve

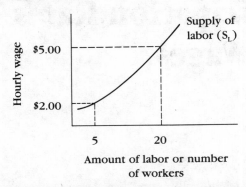

As the wage increases from $2.00/hour to $5.00/hour, people are willing to offer more labor to the market. This was proposed as a general description of labor supply, describing anyone's behavior, male or female.

When economists attempted to explain married *women's* labor force participation rates, however, they changed this model significantly. They added two new elements: family decision making (a big departure from the usual individualistic models) and housework. It is supposed to work as follows. The family sits down and assesses the relative productivity of each family member in market work and housework, and the value of leisure time to each person. These relative productivities are mapped out against the household's needs: cash income, housework to be performed, and leisure. Then the rational household decides how to allocate each person's time. Assume, for instance, the potential wages shown in Table 4-1.

TABLE 4-1
Sample Wages for a Family

	Husband's Worth	Wife's Worth
Market work	$10.00/hour	$5.00/hour
Housework	$2.00/hour	$3.00/hour
Leisure	$6.00/hour	$6.00/hour

Notice that we have assumed that wage discrimination exists in the market; specifically, we have assumed that the husband can earn twice what his wife can earn in market work. Also, we have assumed that women are more productive in housework than men, but that both husband's and wife's leisure time is of equal subjective value.

Suppose the husband and wife estimate that they need $400/week to meet expenses and 40 hours/week of housework to maintain themselves. Then they would rationally allocate their labor as in Table 4-2. Note that the family sends the husband to the labor market to earn the $400/week of needed income, since he is relatively more efficient at labor market work. His wife will perform the housework, since she is relatively more efficient at that. Even if the wife could earn the same market wage as her husband, the model would still indicate that she should stay at home with the housework.

The family could try another option, however. They could hire a household worker to do housework, provided *that* wage is less than the husband's or wife's wage. Following the same model, if the household worker's wages were $3.50/hour, the husband and wife could both take labor market jobs and hire the household worker to do the housework, thereby increasing the family's well-being.

Does anything seem wrong with this simple model of wives' labor force participation? First of all, the model is a bit unrealistic. What family really decides who will do the housework in this fashion? Total role flexibility is implied here. That is, according to the model, if relative wages were reversed, work *roles* would also be reversed. Furthermore, it is assumed that housework and leisure time are separable, an assumption not supported by empirical studies of household work.

Even if economists can defend their positions against most of those objections, their model of household decision making breaks down when the question of women's "double burden" is raised. Women who do market work typically do most of the housework, too, regardless of anyone's relative productivity. Employed wives enjoy leisure time as much as everyone else, but they usually do the

---

TABLE 4-2
The Family's Allocation of Labor

	Husband's Time	Wife's Time
Market work	40 hours/week	0 hours/week
Housework	0 hours/week	40 hours/week
Leisure	72 hours/week	72 hours/week

housework instead. Thus, rather than assuming that household choices are really made in the fashion portrayed by the model, it seems much more straightforward to assume that wives, like all other women and men, enter the labor market because they need the money to meet their expenses.

Economic necessity often does more than push people into the labor market to find jobs. It may mean they take more than one job; they moonlight. It is interesting that the proportion of female moonlighters nearly doubled in recent years.[1] While 16% of all reported moonlighters were female in 1969, women accounted for 30% of all moonlighters by 1979. Why do women, with all the housework to do in addition, take on more than one paid job? In surveys of moonlighters, interviewers have asked them their primary reason for taking an extra job. Almost 20% of the white male moonlighters take more than one job because they "enjoy the work"; less than 30% do it to "meet regular expenses." Turning to black women moonlighters, less than 4% take extra jobs because they "enjoy the work"; over 45% moonlight "to meet regular expenses." Given women's low wages and the double discrimination faced by black women, it is not surprising women take extra jobs just to meet their normal living costs. We return again, then, to the question of women's low wages. Why, as we saw in Figure 1-5 (page 16), is the wage gap not closing, given all the campaign promises and government laws? As a first step in answering this question, we will explore the economists' theories of wage determination and wage discrimination.

Wage Determination: The Demand for Labor and the Supply of Labor

The neoclassical theory of wage determination (the theory used by most modern economists) starts by making certain key assumptions about the nature of labor markets. Labor markets are assumed to be perfectly competitive, which means they are large enough so that no buyers or sellers of labor can exert undue pressure on the market. It is also assumed that all parties in the labor market are well informed and are trying to act rationally, in their own best interests.

The employers enter the market expressing a "demand for labor": they need to employ labor to produce goods. Specifically, their "demand for labor" is a function of their estimation of the "mar-

FIGURE 4-2
The Labor-Demand Curve

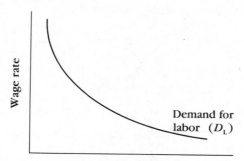

Amount of labor or number of workers

ginal physical productivity" (MPP_L) of that labor (that is, the extra product that an additional worker would produce). It is conventionally assumed that although each extra worker's contribution to output is positive, additional workers will contribute proportionately less to the production output.

Thus, the employers' "demand for labor" is essentially a relation between the wage that is paid and the quantity of labor that should be hired. As you would expect, at higher wages employers will want fewer workers, and at lower wages they will hire more workers. As shown in Figure 4-2, this demand-for-labor curve is therefore downward sloping.

FIGURE 4-3
The Labor-Supply Curve

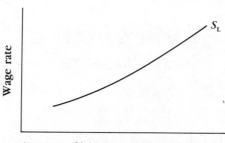

Amount of labor or number of workers

FIGURE 4-4
The Supply-Demand Intersection

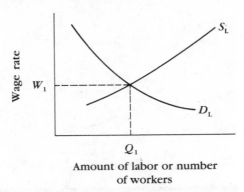

Amount of labor or number
of workers

It is assumed that when workers enter the labor market, they try to decide how much labor to offer to the market and how much time they will keep for themselves as leisure (the so-called labor–leisure choice). If the wage rates are high, workers should be willing to offer more labor to the market; if the wage rates are low, they will offer less labor and prefer more leisure. So workers, too, are deciding how much labor to offer relative to the wage, as shown in Figure 4-3. Note that this is the same supply-of-labor curve given earlier.

According to this simple theory, then, employers and workers can enter the labor market and arrive at a mutually satisfactory wage rate and amount of labor, as shown in Figure 4-4. This figure represents the simplest model of wage determination. But to return to our original question, why women earn less than men, we have to complicate this model, since in the figure *everyone* earns wage W_1.

From Wage Determination to Wage Discrimination: Manipulating the Demand-for-Labor Curve

There are several methods of elaborating this wage determination model, and we will try each one in turn. First, let us examine the "demand for labor." We shall assume that the marginal physical pro-

FIGURE 4-5
A Proposed Model for Explaining Male/Female Wage Differences: Different Demand Curves

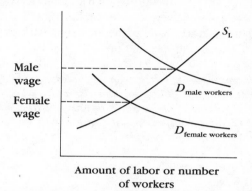

Amount of labor or number
of workers

duce of *female* workers is less than the marginal physical product of *male* workers. How could this be? One frequently heard reply is that women may invest less in their "human capital" than men. Perhaps women have less training or education, either because they plan shorter careers in the labor market and want less training or because they are discriminated against in their *access* to education or training. The net result would be that the MPP$_L$ of women is less than that of men, so that the demand for women's labor (which is a *function* of this MPP$_L$) is less than the demand for men's labor, and the wage for women lower than the wage for men, as shown in Figure 4-5. But statistical evidence indicates that women are just as well educated as men, averaging 12½ years of schooling, which makes the assumption that women have invested less in their human capital somewhat unsatisfactory.[2]

Some economists have offered an alternative assumption. They argue that women's productivity is less than men's because women's absenteeism and turnover rates on the job are higher than men's. According to available data, occupational mobility rates for males and females are roughly the same. Job-tenure rates (length of time spent with the same employer)[3] for both, however, indicate that males have a slightly longer average job tenure. Should this be interpreted as an indication that women's MPP$_L$ is less than men's, on the average?

To answer this question, we must examine the question of causality. Is high job turnover a function of the worker or the type of job?

For example, the manager of a grocery store, with a good salary and daily responsibilities, may have more incentive to come to work regularly and keep that job than would the supermarket cashier. Some jobs, particularly low-paying jobs, may have high turnover and absenteeism "built in." If predominantly women and minority workers have been hired for these relatively less desirable jobs, we may be mistakenly applying the characteristics of the *job* to the workers themselves. The Bureau of Labor Statistics cautions us:

> *. . . in the manufacturing sector, women tended to have higher quit rates than men, partially because industries with a high proportion of women employed are also among the lower-paying ones. Hence, part of the reason for differences in quit propensities between the sexes is the concentration of women in lower-paying jobs.*[4]

In effect, they are suggesting that high quit rates are a *result,* not a *cause,* of low wages.

Ultimately, all these explanations of the differing MPP_L of males and females suffer from a basic problem. Since we cannot really *measure* the MPP_L of anyone, it is hard to prove that it explains different demand-for-labor curves. Still, staying with demand-side models, we can try another approach: the famous economic theories of discrimination. We start by assuming that women's MPP_L is equal to men's MPP_L. But now the employer's demand for labor is not just a function of the MPP_L; it is also a function of the pleasure he derives from discriminating against different types of employees (preferring whites over blacks, men over women, and so on). Thus the new demand-for-labor curve is determined by two variables, the MPP_L and the employer's "taste for discrimination." The graph of this model might be that of Figure 4-5, but since we assume that the MPP_L's of the males and females are equal, the distance between the two labor-demand curves is the employer's taste for discrimination. Women's wages here are less than their productivity, or their MPP_L.

The crux of the model is that for the discriminating employer, there is a trade-off between his pleasure from discriminating and his production profits. He could raise his profits (or cut his losses, as the case may be) by hiring more women up to the higher wage that their productivity justifies. This, in fact, is supposed to be the downfall of the discriminator. A market in which there is competition will attract manufacturers who do not care about the pleasure of discriminating, but only about the pleasure of profits. They will hire fewer of the relatively expensive men and offer women higher wages, and earn higher profits than the discriminators. Under competition, the higher-profit nondiscriminators will force the lower-profit discriminators out of business. The moral of this story is that in the long run, competitive markets will not tolerate profits being sacrificed for the pleasures of discrimination. The economists who constructed these models of discrimination anxiously awaited the time series evidence that would show the gradual improvement of women's wages under competition. Confronted with the widening wage gap data (Figure 1-5, page 16), discrimination-theory economists have had to reevaluate their data bases and admit to weaknesses in the theory.

Wage Discrimination: Manipulating the Supply-of-Labor Curve

Let us try the "supply side" of economic theory. We shall assume a single demand curve for female and male labor (returning to the idea that female and male MPP_L's are the same), but differing *supply* curves, such that female wages are lower than male wages (Figure 4-6). Since we know that anyone's supply-of-labor curve is supposed to be determined by the person's labor–leisure choice, this model assumes that women value their leisure less than men and thus are willing to supply their labor to the market at lower wages.

FIGURE 4-6
A Proposed Model for Explaining Male/Female Wage Differences: Different Supply Curves

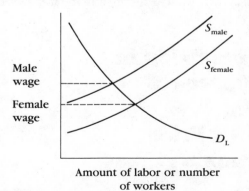

Amount of labor or number of workers

When you think about it, though, why should women value their leisure less than men? One obvious reason is that women enjoy less leisure, since women, unlike men, spend most of their "leisure" doing housework. Economists find this explanation of women's lower labor-supply curve rather tricky, since by reminding us that women's labor is *also* productive in housework, it might mean that women could charge higher wages than men for entering the paid labor market. This higher female labor-supply curve should mean higher wages for women.

Wage Discrimination in a "Job Crowding" Model

Are there any other explanations for a separate and higher labor-supply curve for men? We could return to the idea we tried to use on the demand side, that men have invested more in their human capital; thus they could ask for proportionately higher wages for themselves. Alternatively, we could turn to a theory of "job crowding." Here we inject a note of realism as we posit that not all jobs are the same. Specifically, we assume that (because of past discrimination or cultural norms) most women are trying to enter a relatively small number of typically female occupations, while males supply their labor to any occupation. This produces a relative oversupply of females to a more limited job sector, which reduces women's wages relative to men's, as shown by the separate demand curves in Figure 4-5. Thus, we could assume a separate demand curve (as well as a separate supply curve) for the "crowded" occupations, as in Figure 4-7. While this "job crowding" hypothesis makes some intuitive sense, it clearly will not explain why women and men in the *same* jobs would earn different wages.

Wage Discrimination in Models of Imperfect Competition: Oligopsonistic Price Discrimination

We have juggled models without much success so far, in that we have not found a model based on reasonable assumptions (such as women's MPP_L = men's MPP_L) that also predicts a stable, profit-

FIGURE 4-7
A Proposed Model for Explaining Male/Female Wage Differences: Different Demand and Supply Curves

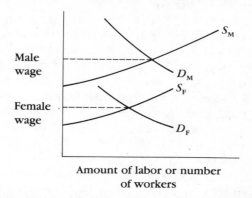

maximizing outcome with male wages higher than female wages. We may improve our chances if we abandon the assumption of perfect competition in labor markets. Specifically, the economists' "oligopsonistic price discrimination" model describes a situation much like the "company town" where there are only a few employers facing a labor force that can be sorted out and paid different wage rates based on different labor-supply characteristics. If there is one employer, for instance, and he knows that the males will offer their labor in a different pattern from that of the females, he can offer each group a separate wage that maximizes his profits overall. This price-discriminating oligopsonist uses his control over employment opportunities, combines it with his knowledge that the labor-supply curve for males and females are different, and manages to pay each group different wages. He thereby makes maximum profits and ensures his long-run viability in the market.

An example may make this model clearer. Consider the case of a small town with only one major employer, a college. The college hires mostly men for its faculty positions, with perhaps a few women. They pay these professors a competitive wage to attract them to come to the town to work. Assume that many of these professors are married, and that their wives may need employment. The only major employer in the area, however, is the college. The college personnel office, realizing they have a captive audience, offers these wives low-wage jobs, at rates below what they could earn in other cities. The faculty wives might accept these low-wage positions, knowing they have few other choices. This is a dramatic example of the ability of a single employer (a monopsonist) to maximize profits by using market power. In a similar vein, a small group of employers (oligopsonists) might successfully offer higher wages to males than females for the *same* jobs, assuming they can judge the wage sensitivity of the males and females accurately.

Since this model involves fairly complex information about the labor-supply characteristics of different groups of workers, it is quite complicated. Yet the basic dynamics of the model begin to conform more to what most people find reasonable: that discrimination *is* profitable and that employers enter the market with some degree of power over the wage bargaining process (unlike our earlier models with no long-run profits to be made from discriminating and with perfect competition between buyers and sellers of labor).

Some useful insights emerge from this type of model. Discriminatory wages are now seen as the outcome of power struggles in the labor market, rather than as a result of the forces of perfect competition. Employers, well aware of past and present discrimination against women, offer women lower wages than men—not because they feel women's productivity is less than men's, but because they can use the social fact of discrimination to offer women less pay. Women accept lower wages because they need an income to survive and because they have not had the market power (lacking union support, for instance) to enable them to bargain for more. With bargaining power, women's wages improve considerably. A recent study showed, for instance, that the median income of union women was 30% higher than the median income of nonunion women.[5] We shall analyze this figure in more detail in Chapter 10, but the point should be clear: While wages obviously bear a relation to worker productivity, productivity is not the only factor or even the most important factor that determines wages. Market power, in contrast, not only seems to be a more *reasonable* way to explain how wages are set, but also enables us to see how discrimination can exist and endure in labor markets. With less organization, women have had less power in the wage struggle, and thus lower wages.

Additional Readings

For a good, general review of the history of economic thought on women, readers should try to locate J. Madden, "The Development of Economic Thought on the Woman Problem," *Review of Radical Political Economics,* Summer 1972. For an anthology of economists' papers on women's wages, see A. Amsden, ed., *Economics of Women and Work* (Penguin, 1980). For a good discussion of the issue of wage differences in particular, Mary Stevenson's "Wage Differences between Men and Women: Economic Theories," in Stromberg and Harkess, *Women Working* (Mayfield, 1978) is excellent. Skeptical readers, who may find this account of neoclassical wage theory somewhat incredible, are advised to consult any principles of economics or labor economics textbook for confirmation. For a general critique of this wage theory, readers may wish to consult B. Berch, "Wages and Labour," in *Economics: An Anti-Text* (Macmillan Press, London, 1977).

Notes

1. Sckscenski, E., "Women's Share of Moonlighting Nearly Doubles During 1969–1979," *Monthly Labor Review,* May 1980, pp. 36–39.

2. *1975 Handbook on Women Workers,* p. 183.

3. *Ibid,* pp. 61, 63.

4. *Ibid,* p. 61.

5. Women's Bureau, *Employment Goals of the World Plan of Action: Developments and Issues in the United States,* p. 11.

Labor Market Work: Occupational Distribution

In the preceding chapter, we did not discuss one of the most common "explanations" of women's low wages: that women work in low-paying jobs. While the observation may be accurate, it hardly *explains* low wages; it is really only a tautology. Yet we can observe that women are not randomly distributed in the occupational structure. The sex segregation of the labor market is such an important aspect of women's work experience that we should examine it in detail here.

What Are Pink-Collar Jobs?

In 1979, about half of all employed women were working in less than 30 of the approximately 419 detailed census occupations; in these occupations, 80% or more of the workers were women.[1] Which occupations are these? From Table 1-4 (see page 14) we know the sectors of the economy where most women workers are located: 55.3% of all employed women are in clerical or service work. To know which occupations within those (and other) sectors are female dominated, we need to consult Table 5-1, which provides a finer breakdown of the various occupations in each sector.

Some interesting insights can be gained from this data. A broad occupational category such as "Operators" may appear sexually mixed (32.0% female), yet *within* the occupational category, the actual occupations are very sex segregated. Operators include "sewers and stitchers" (95.3% female) and "truck drivers" (2.1% female). It is

TABLE 5-1
Women as a Percentage of Total Employment in Selected Occupations: 1974–1979
(Numbers in Thousands)

Occupation	1979		1978		1977	
	Total employment	Women as a Percentage of the Total	Total Employment	Women as a Percentage of the Total	Total Employment	Women as a Percentage of the Total
Professional and technical	15,050	43.3	14,245	42.7	13,692	42.6
Accountants	1,045	32.9	975	30.1	868	27.5
Computer specialists	534	26.0	428	23.1	371	23.2
Industrial engineers	245	7.3	206	8.7	214	7.0
Lawyers and judges	499	12.4	499	9.4	462	9.5
Librarians	188	80.9	187	84.5	193	83.4
Life and physical scientists	280	18.9	273	17.9	275	15.6
Physicians	431	10.7	424	11.3	403	11.2
Registered nurses	1,223	96.8	1,112	96.7	1,063	96.7
Elementary teachers	1,374	84.3	1,304	84.0	1,313	84.2
Secondary teachers	1,213	50.7	1,154	51.6	1,157	51.2
Surveyors	85	3.5	82	2.4	68	1.5
Airplane pilots	72	—	69	1.4	64	—
Managers and administrators	10,516	24.6	10.105	23.4	9,662	22.3
Bank officials and financial managers	620	31.6	573	30.4	543	27.3
School administrators (elementary and secondary)	299	37.5	275	35.6	265	36.2
Clerical workers	17,613	80.3	16,904	79.6	16,106	78.9
Typists	1,020	96.7	1,044	96.6	1,006	96.3
Craft and kindred workers	12,880	5.7	12,386	5.6	11,881	5.0
Carpenters	1,276	1.3	1,253	1.0	1,171	.9
Painters, construction and maintenance	483	5.0	484	5.2	461	3.3
Machinists and job setters	642	3.3	591	3.0	576	2.6
Auto mechanics	1,272	.6	1,209	.6	1,161	.9
Printing craft workers	455	22.2	417	21.8	389	22.4
Telephone installers and repairers	302	9.9	297	6.7	279	5.0

[a]Percent not shown where employment estimate is less than 35,000.

TABLE 5-1 *(continued)*
Women as a Percentage of Total Employment in Selected Occupations: 1974–1979 (Numbers in Thousands)

1976		1975		1974		
Total Employment	Women as a Percentage of the Total	Total Employment	Women as a Percentage of the Total	Total Employment	Women as a Percentage of the Total	Percent change 1975–1979
13,329	42.0	12,748	41.3	12,338	40.5	23.8
866	26.9	782	24.6	803	23.7	79.2
387	19.1	363	21.2	311	19.0	80.5
201	4.5	187	2.7	193	—a	260.0
413	9.2	392	7.1	359	7.0	121.4
183	82.4	180	81.1	N.A.	N.A.	4.1
282	12.1	277	14.4	246	15.9	32.5
368	12.8	354	13.0	346	9.8	—
999	96.6	935	97.0	904	98.0	30.5
1,383	84.8	1,332	85.4	1,297	84.3	1.8
1,188	50.5	1,184	49.2	1,186	48.3	5.5
69	1.4	70	—	N.A.	N.A.	—
64	—	60	—	N.A.	N.A.	—
9,315	20.8	8,891	19.4	8,941	18.5	49.9
546	24.7	518	23.6	510	21.4	60.7
282	32.6	263	28.1	352	27.8	51.4
15,558	78.7	15,128	77.8	15,043	77.6	20.2
983	96.7	1,025	96.6	1,038	96.2	.4
11,278	4.8	10,972	4.6	11,477	4.5	46.1
1,021	.7	988	.6	1,073	—a	183.3
413	2.9	420	3.8	456	—a	50.0
570	2.9	557	2.5	558	—a	50.0
1,124	.6	1,102	.5	1,041	—a	33.3
380	19.2	375	17.6	386	18.1	53.3
282	5.0	314	4.8	349	4.9	100.0

(continued)

TABLE 5-1 *(continued)*
Women as a Percentage of Total Employment in Selected Occupations:
1974–1979 (Numbers in Thousands)

Occupation	1979		1978		1977	
	Total employment	Women as a Percentage of the Total	Total Employment	Women as a Percentage of the Total	Total Employment	Women as a Percentage of the Total
Operators, including transport	14,521	32.0	14,416	31.7	13,830	31.4
Meat cutters and butchers, manufacturing	89	31.5	114	28.9	88	35.2
Punch and stamping press operators	158	29.1	156	30.1	152	36.2
Sewers and stitchers	810	95.3	814	94.8	820	95.2
Bus drivers	358	45.5	337	45.1	339	42.2
Truck drivers	1,965	2.1	1,923	1.9	1,898	1.3
Service workers	12,834	62.4	12,839	62.6	12,392	62.0
Cleaners and servants	485	97.3	530	97.0	574	96.5
Waiters	1,363	89.4	1,383	90.5	1,310	90.4
Nursing aides, orderlies	1,024	87.5	1,037	87.0	1,008	86.3
Hairdressers and cosmetologists	575	89.2	542	89.1	526	88.2
Protective service workers	1,406	8.8	1,358	8.5	1,324	7.9

[a]Percent not shown where employment estimate is less than 35,000.

Source: U.S. Department of Labor, Bureau of Labor Statistics, Employment and Earnings, June 1975 and January 197
1977, 1978, 1979, and 1980.

important, then, to be aware of the sex segregation of jobs *within* sectors as well as the overall distribution of women across sectors. If we focus on some of the major female-dominated occupations and study their composition over the past few years (Table 5-2), we can see how remarkably constant they have been.

Sexual divisions of the labor market apply to most women, regardless of ethnic background, as Table 5-3 reveals. Apart from a few exceptions (the high concentration of Filipino-American women in professional work, Puerto-Rican and Cuban women as factory operatives, and black women in services), women of very different ethnic backgrounds work in the same "pink collar ghetto."

Should this handful of female occupations really be called a ghetto? Doesn't that imply a rather unpleasant or undesirable state of affairs? Perhaps women *prefer* to work in those few occupations. Yet

Table 5-1 *(continued)*
Women as Percentage of Total Employment in Selected
Occupations: 1974–1979 (Numbers in Thousands)

1976		1975		1974		
Total Employment	Women as a Percentage of the Total	Total Employment	Women as a Percentage of the Total	Total Employment	Women as a Percentage of the Total	Percent change 1975–1979
13,356	31.2	12,856	30.2	13,919	31.1	19.6
87	29.9	100	27.0	N.A.	N.A.	3.7
155	32.9	130	27.7	170	30.6	27.8
812	95.9	803	95.8	858	95.8	.4
332	39.5	310	37.7	265	37.4	39.3
1,741	1.2	1,694	1.1	1,752	—[a]	121.1
12,005	61.5	11,657	62.3	11,373	62.9	10.3
553	97.1	599	97.3	588	97.6	−23.5
1,259	90.7	1,183	91.1	1,182	91.8	13.1
1,002	86.8	1,001	85.8	959	86.9	4.3
534	88.0	504	90.5	498	92.4	12.5
1,302	6.4	1,290	6.3	1,254	6.4	51.2

this suggestion of preference implies choice. Can it really be argued that women *choose* this small range of occupations when so few others seem open to women? The high degree of established sex segregation of jobs must affect the choices of young women more than those of young men, who observe a wider range of occupations among which to choose. Most people's labor market choices are affected by what they see possible in the market already.

Pink Collar = Low Pay

Beyond the issue of a smaller range of occupational choices, however, there is a more fundamental problem with sex segregation of jobs. As is often true in ghettos, conditions are not ideal. Specifically,

TABLE 5-2
Proportion of Employed Workers Who Were Women in Each of the Selected Occupations for Selected Years Since 1960

Occupation	1975[1]	1974[2]	1973[3]	1970[4]	1960[4]
All occupations	39.0	33.9	38.4	37.7	32.8
Nurses, dieticians, therapists		93.1		94.4	96.0
Registered nurses		98.0	97.8	97.3	97.5
Teachers, except college	70.6	69.2	69.9	70.2	72.6
Elementary school teachers		84.3	84.5	83.6	85.8
Salesworkers, retail trade	61.6	60.9			
Sales clerks, retail trade		69.4	69.0	64.6	63.3
Bookkeepers		89.2	88.3	82.0	83.4
Cashiers		87.7	86.7	83.5	76.9
Secretaries, typists, and stenographers	98.4	98.4		96.6	96.5
Secretaries			99.1	97.6	97.1
Typists			96.6	94.2	95.1
Operatives, except transport	39.5	40.4	39.2	37.9	35.5
Sewers and stitchers			95.5	93.7	94.0
Food service workers	74.6	74.7	69.7	68.0	67.6
Waiters			82.9	88.8	86.6
Private household workers	98.0	98.2	98.3	96.6	96.4

[1]U.S. Department of Labor, Bureau of Labor Statistics, "Employment and Earnings" (Washington, D.C.: Government Printing Office, January 1976), table 18, p. 146. Employed persons 20 and over; annual averages of monthly data.

[2]Unless otherwise specified, 1974 data are from U.S. Department of Labor, Bureau of Labor Statistics, "Employment and Earnings" (Washington, D.C.: Government Printing Office, June 1975), table 1, p. 7. Annual average of monthly data.

[3]U.S. Department of Labor, "1975 Handbook on Women Workers" (Washington, D.C.: Government Printing Office, 1976), pp. 89–91. Annual averages of monthly data.

[4]U.S. Department of Commerce, Bureau of the Census, 1970 Census of Population, "Detailed Characteristics of the Population: U.S. Summary" (Washington, D.C.: Government Printing Office, 1973), table 221. Employed persons 14 years old and over, pp. 718.

women's wages are lower in the pink-collar ghetto than outside. Referring back to Table 1-4, we can see that women's major occupational groups—clerical and service work—are low-wage sectors of the economy. Even if we find women who "prefer" those pink-collar jobs, it is doubtful that we will find women who prefer low-paying work, a basic characteristic of this ghetto.

While the basic wages in pink-collar jobs are low, wage inequity seems to be worse in male-dominated occupations; that is, the female/male earnings ratios are lower in male-intensive jobs than in female-intensive jobs. For example, elementary school teaching is 84% female and women in that occupation earn 86% of what their male colleagues earn (see Table 5-4). Medical and osteopathic physicians,

TABLE 5-3
Percentage of Employed Women in Each Sector

Ethnic Group	Professional	Managerial	Sales	Clerical	Craft	Operative	Non-Farm Labor	Non-Household Service	Private Service Work
White	16	4	6	37	2	14	1	14	2
Black	11	1	3	21	1	17	1	25	18
Mexican-American	6	2	6	26	2	26	2	21	5
Puerto Rican	7	2	4	30	2	40	1	12	1
Cuban-American	9	1	5	26	3	43	1	11	1
American-Indian	11	2	4	25	2	19	1	26	7
Japanese-American	16	4	7	34	2	13	1	17	4
Chinese-American	19	4	5	32	1	23	1	13	2
Filipino-American	32	2	4	29	1	11	1	17	2

Source: E. Almquist and J. Wehrle-Einhorn, pp. 68, 69.

on the other hand, are only 13% female and those women earn only 41% of what men earn. Overall, statisticians have found that the female/male earnings ratios average .50 in male-dominated occupations (0–20% female), .55 in neutral occupations (21–59% female), and .62 in female-dominated occupations (60–100% female).[2] The only exception to this pattern seems to be the black women in female-dominated occupations, who have some of the lowest-paying jobs in the female ghetto.[3] (In contrast to the overall statistics, black women's earnings relative to black men's improve in male-dominated occupations.) This statistical finding is yet another illustration of what "doubly disadvantaged" means for minority women in our labor force.

So far, we have only described the sex segregation of jobs. We have identified which sectors and which occupations are female dominated. We have seen that jobs in the pink-collar ghetto are low paid, even if women face less wage discrimination in these occupations than in the male-dominated ones. Our next step, then, is to examine the *dynamics* of sex segregation.

How Sex Segregation Works: Vertical Segregation

To simplify matters, we will first look at sex segregation *within* occupations, usually termed *vertical* segregation. That is, we will examine the sex distribution of workers in any single occupation, to see if males characteristically hold the upper level jobs and females the lower level jobs within that occupation. For instance, among sales workers, the highest-paying work is in commissioned, non-retail sales, where men predominate. Even in retail sales, men hold the better-paying jobs, selling the "big ticket" commissioned items, while women sell the lower-priced items and earn less.[4]

When some economists discovered the pervasiveness of vertical segregation, they developed a model of how it seems to operate, a theory of "internal labor markets." They found that in many modern firms there are at least two labor markets in operation, a primary and a secondary market. Primary market positions are characterized by high pay, good working conditions, promotion ladders, fringe benefits, and good job security. The secondary market jobs, on the other hand, are characterized by low pay, poor working conditions, few fringe benefits, and little job security. These are the "dead end" jobs, which are filled by continually recruiting new workers from what is seen as a casual labor pool. As these analysts picture it, both labor

TABLE 5-4

Occupation	Women as % of All Workers	1975 Median Earning Female	1975 Median Earning Male	Women's Pay Men's Pay
Kindergarten and pre-kindergarten teachers	99	$ 9,348	—	—
Waiters and waitresses	93	4,441	$ 6,027	.74
Bookkeepers	92	7,455	12,300	.61
Cashiers	91	5,973	10,553	.57
Elementary school teachers	84	10,545	12,243	.86
Miscellaneous clerical workers	82	7,710	10,220	.75
Insurance agents/brokers	15	$ 8,758	$14,947	.59
Managers and administrators	15	8,445	16,657	.51
Medical and osteopathic doctors	13	14,893	35,960	.41
Blue collar work supervisors	10	7,832	14,297	.55

Source: N. Rytina, p. 51, "Occupational Segregation and Earnings Differences by Sex," *Monthly Labor Review,* January 1981, p. 49.

markets exist in any given firm, side by side, but workers do not commonly move from one market to the other. Rather, they are usually assigned to one or the other market by their employers on the basis of race, age, or sex. This assignment then becomes a self-fulfilling prophecy: women or blacks offered secondary market jobs have little reason to treat the job as permanent, or worth holding onto for a long time. This description of the structure of internal labor markets is useful for understanding the patterns of vertical segregation, even if it suggests few ways to eliminate the problem. Less bias in personnel offices would clearly help. Similarly, a policy of "job posting," where *all* vacancies in a firm are advertised to the *entire* staff, helps to break down segregated job ladders within firms.

How Can We Explain the Sex Segregation of Occupations?

Surrounding this vertical sex segregation of jobs within firms is the *horizontal* sex segregation of the whole labor market, that is, the disproportionate concentration of women in certain occupations and their absence from other jobs. Horizontal sex segregation is easier to describe than to explain. Why does this pink-collar ghetto exist? Some people might argue that it is natural, that it simply reflects certain basic characteristics of women's "nature." They would say that the secretary is usually female, for example, because the work reflects women's basic nature. Helpful, supportive, and efficient, the secretary is the "office wife." These people offer similar explanations for women nurses or office cleaners. It is not really obvious why typing office memos, scrubbing office floors, or emptying bed pans are inherently ladylike activities, or functions related to women's basic nature, but the real problem with this nonexplanation is even more fundamental.

Let us take a look at the history of women's occupational distribution in America. While women in the nineteenth century were widely employed as servants, recall that women were also considered the "natural" choice to be the first factory workers in America. Our first industrial revolution relied on these women workers. Throughout the nineteenth century, women retained a key role in our basic industries, as the figures in Table 5-5 reveal.

Women workers used to predominate in the clothing industries and in cotton textile manufacturing. They also had a strong foothold in boot and shoe manufacturing, and they had an increasing share of the work in printing, publishing, and cigar/cigarette production. Occupations were sex segregated, but women were segregated into *different* occupations. After the Civil War, for instance, the majority of teachers and nurses were women; yet in 1870 women were only 3.3% of the office workers, and by 1890 they were still less than 17% of all office workers.[5]

TABLE 5-5
Sectoral Distribution of Women in the U.S. Labor Force: 1831–1905

Sector	Percentage of Women Out of All Workers Employed							
	1831	1850	1860	1870	1880	1890	1900	1905
Cigars and cigarettes			9	10	17	28	37	42
Factory, boot and shoe					23	30	33	33
Men's clothing		62	63	55	54	44	46	
Women's clothing		85	88	88	66	67	63	
Book and job printing					12	19	20	23
Printing and publishing						14	18	20
Cotton	68	64	62	60	57	54	49	47
All industries		24	21	18	22	20	21	

Source: E. Abbott, *Women in Industry,* 1919, pp. 102–360. Data for each sector taken from the following pages, respectively: 195, 178, 234, 241, 259, 102, and 360.

In other words, the appropriateness of various occupations for women and men has been quite different in different historical periods. There is nothing "natural" about it. Furthermore, even in modern times, the actual sex labeling of occupations differs across cultures. For example, three-fourths of all physicians in the Soviet Union are women, and similar figures could be cited for Israel.[6] In many African communities, women have monopolized the trading occupations.

While the sex label on various occupations differs over time and across cultures, one basic characteristic of the female jobs rarely changes at all: female-dominated occupations are almost invariably the lowest-paid jobs. In Table 5-6 we can see that in the Soviet Union, for example, the highest-income occupations are male intensive and the lowest paid are female intensive.

Once we realize that the sex labeling of jobs varies over time and doesn't just reflect women's essential nature or character, we can start to examine the dynamics of this sex segregation of occupations. As our examination of the history of women's participation in the labor force suggested, women's movements into different occupations in America have been profoundly shaped by the types of technology employers have used and by trade union struggles over access to particular jobs. As we have seen, male workers, particularly in the post-Civil War period, felt doubly insecure. First, urbanization and industrialization spelled the decline of independent craftwork, and dependence on factory employment, even for men. Second, increased mechanization and technological change threatened to erode skilled

TABLE 5-6
Women's Participation in the Labor Force and Their Earnings: Soviet Union, 1975

Sector	Women as Percentage of Labor Force	Average Monthly Wage (Rubles)
Construction	29	159.4
Transport	24	150.8
Science and science services	49	143.6
Education and culture	73	112.7
Agriculture	44	111.8
Public health, physical culture, and social welfare	85	95.3

Source: G. Lapidus, "Occupational Segregation and Public Policy: A Comparative Analysis of American and Soviet Patterns," *in* M. Blaxall and B. Reagan, *Women and the Workplace,* p. 133.

workers' control over the jobs. Their bosses could replace them, either with immigrant workers or with women workers. So unions reacted in the face of this offensive. Union members figured that if women, blacks, and new immigrants could be excluded from competition for their jobs, they would have more security. They tried to exclude women from union membership (or they bargained with their employers to exclude women) and they lobbied for protective legislation to bar women from various types of jobs. Of course, they couched their strategy in romantic terms, arguing that the job control they would win would yield them better wages, which would mean their wives wouldn't have to work. But since women still needed to work, this strategy meant only that women workers were pushed into other sectors of the economy—services, clerical work, and some white-collar professions. The modern female ghetto should be seen, then, as the result of an *exclusion* process, not as a natural, ahistorical phenomenon.

The Breakdown of Segregation

Is this situation changing now? Recent television specials about women coal miners and assembly-line workers give us the impression that the walls of the ghetto are finally crumbling. Yet the data on women's progress into male-intensive occupations does not support this media impression, at least for the decade of the 1960s. If we look at the proportion of women workers in the male-intensive occupations (fields where over 75% of the workers are male), we find that these women were 13.5% of all women workers in 1960 and 15% in 1970.[7] The difference is not terribly impressive. Indeed, we need to examine this "progress" in more detail. Are women moving into all of the various male-dominated occupations or just into the traditionally male jobs being abandoned by men in favor of better jobs? Some clues can be found by consulting Table 5-7, where various male-intensive occupations are listed, with their growth rates of female employment and their overall rates of growth.

Presumably, occupations with overall employment growth are more promising and dynamic than those experiencing shrinkage. The healthy growth (18%) of female technicians is probably a good sign, since the field itself is expanding (856.4%). Yet women also may be moving into many declining occupations (shoe repair, baking, and weighing), which apparently are being abandoned by men. Thus, women may be penetrating some of the less dynamic male-intensive occupations, although the evidence is not really clear.

TABLE 5-7
**Male-Intensive Occupations With a Large Increase in the
Female Share of Employment: 1960–1970**

	MI Class[a]	Percentage Point Increase in the Female Share: 1960–1970	Percent Change in Total Employment: 1960–1970
Actuaries	VMI	20	71.7
Tool programmers	VMI	14	47.6
Technicians, not elsewhere classified	VMI	18	856.4
Accountants	MMI	10	43.7
College teachers, math	MMI	18	137.6
Radio operators	MMI	12	60.5
Bank officers/financial managers	VMI	9	1,195.6
Sales, services and construction	MMI	11	13.1
Bill and account collectors	MMI	16	57.8
Expediters	MMI	9	41.7
Insurance adjusters	MMI	15	71.5
Postal clerks	MMI	13	30.6
Ticket agents	MMI	15	33.7
Weighers	MMI	10	−8.2
Dental laboratory technicians	VMI	18	78.2
Furniture finishers	VMI	13	2.9
Shoe repairers	VMI	14	−24.4
Bakers	MMI	12	−2.7
Engravers	MMI	9	22.1
Bus drivers	VMI	18	29.9
Bartenders	MMI	11	9.9

[a](Male intensive) means that 75 or more percent of employment in the occupation was male, VMI (very male intensive) means 90 or more percent, and MMI (moderately male intensive) means that 75–89 percent were male.

Source: U.S. Bureau of the Census, Census of the Population, 1970. "Detailed Characteristics, PC(1)-D1, U.S. Summary" (Washington, D.C.: Government Printing Office, 1973), Table 221.

What about the prestigious male-intensive occupations? Let us look at women's progress into management as an example. A 1980 *Wall Street Journal* survey of female business executives indicated that while there are more women executives than ever before, the problem of vertical sex segregation is severe. Most of the female executives are categorized as either corporate secretaries or assistant secretaries. This is reflected in the average salary data: 60% of the female executives earn under $50,000 per year and 30% earn less than $30,000. (The average male executive income was $134,500).[8] Business consultants suggest that the major reason for women's lack of success in management careers is tension between them and their male bosses. As they put it:

> *... some male bosses can't picture women in positions of power and so subconsciously undermine their efforts to advance. They may refuse to let them exercise authority or try to "protect" them by withholding difficult assignments.*[9]

Management's resistance to the entry of women into their ranks seems quite deep seated and effective.

Women who *do* enter these male-dominated occupations may wonder if it was worth the struggle. Recent studies have uncovered the sexual harrassment of women workers, especially in predominantly male work environments. In addition to sexual harrassment, many women entering formerly male jobs find themselves pressured into superhuman productivity as the token woman. Being "the test case" for all of womankind in a largely hostile environment can be rather burdensome.

In the 1980s, however, women in nontraditional jobs face more than sexual harrassment and more than the inflated expectations of tokenism; they face the recessionary layoff. Job cutbacks under the "last-hired, first-fired" rule immediately jeopardize the jobs of all women who benefited from affirmative action hiring programs to take nontraditional jobs in manufacturing. The *Wall Street Journal* reports:

> *Of course, women who not long ago broke tradition by landing high-paying manufacturing jobs on assembly lines found themselves the first to get laid off in the recession. They had less seniority under union rules than men. The share of women in General Motors' hourly work force dropped to 17.3% in August from 18.1% in January. Ford also reports that its hourly women workers were more seriously affected by layoffs than men.*[10]

Since the 1980s recession hit the manufacturing sectors first, its unemployment burden has fallen disproportionately on manufacturing workers—including those new women workers who were supposed to integrate those trades. So while most workers face the threat of losing their jobs in a recession or depression, women workers who have recently entered a traditionally male field (along with any new male workers) are especially vulnerable. Ironically, they get the "cold shoulder" from labor unions as well, since unions defend their seniority rules in layoff procedures. "Last hired, first fired" may indeed be the bottom line in women's struggles to integrate the job structure.

In fact, this whole review of women's occupational segregation suggests that the problem is far more fundamental than statistics tables or tokenism trends would reveal. Why have women had such little success trying to break into the traditionally male jobs? On first thought, male workers are the villains, since they have been saving the best-paid jobs for themselves. But *their* hold on the jobs has been precarious too, which was a primary reason why they thought they needed to exclude women workers in the first place. One underlying problem is that in our economic system, the right to have a job is not guaranteed to any worker, male or female. On the contrary, our labor market system is based on competition among workers, for what may be a shrinking number of jobs as we now reorganize our industrial base. So women's attempts to expand into male-dominated occupations and black workers' attempts to move out of their job ghetto may meet even more resistance in the 1980s. The white male backlash against affirmative action hiring programs may be only the beginning. In defense of their precarious jobs, white males may resist any attempts to fracture the system of race/sex job segmentation.

What could help women workers overcome these difficulties? Clearly, the fundamental problem of labor market competition can only be addressed by an equally fundamental change in our economic system. Within the present economic structure of the United States, several policy options exist. While we shall delve more deeply into government legislation in Chapter 8, we should mention at this point the issue of equal pay laws. The current definition of nondiscrimination, "equal pay for equal work," is certainly just, but it will never offer full economic justice to women working in sex-segregated jobs. Here there may be too few men to become equal with, and these will probably be the low-paid men, since women are concentrated in the low-wage end of the job spectrum. Consequently, women workers have been promoting the concept of "equal pay for work of comparable worth," which would ensure women equal pay for work of basically similar quality. Unfortunately, the business lobbies have blocked this type of legislation. While *any* legislation, including the existing equal-pay acts, suffers from the problem of compliance, it still can be a valuable tool for women workers.

Apart from government legislation, what paths lead out of the pink-collar ghetto? As mentioned earlier, the individualistic solutions (as exemplified by the woman trailblazer making her own way in a male-dominated sector) may present problems of sexual harrassment and the heightened expectations accompanying tokenism. Furthermore, these women may find their "coattails clipped." Rather than bringing other women in, they may find the door to their male-dominated occupation closing behind them.

In general, less individualistic strategies may be more productive. These include job desegregation efforts backed by segments of the women's movement or the trade union movement, which would lessen the individual burden of social change and open up the potential for including more women as beneficiaries of change. Above all, we need to address the process of role socialization taking place in primary and secondary schools. The career guidance given to young people is probably important for their later decisions about the types of work appropriate for males or females.

On this note of guarded optimism, we can conclude our examination of two dimensions of women's labor market work—wages and occupational distribution. We will resume our treatment of these issues in later chapters, when we look at how business, government, and unions view women's work. We turn next to a consideration of two other uses of women's productive labor: housework and childbearing work.

Additional Readings

One of the best collections of articles to consult is M. Blaxall and B. Reagan, eds., *Women and the Workplace: The Implications of Occupational Segregation* (University of Chicago Press, 1976), particularly the article by F. Blau and C. Jusenius, "Economists' Approaches to Sex Segregation in the Labor Market: An Appraisal." For a good alternative formulation, see H. Hartmann's "Capitalism, Patriarchy and Job Segregation by Sex," *in* Z. Eisenstein, ed., *Capitalist Patriarchy and the Case for Socialist Feminism* (Monthly Review Press, 1979). Also, Louise Kapp Howe's *Pink Collar Workers* (Avon, 1978) is an excellent book, full of interviews with women workers. Reading the comments of the women she talks with will give you a better sense of the dimensions of the female ghetto.

Notes

1. N. Rytina, "Occupational Segregation and Earnings Differences by Sex," *Monthly Labor Review,* January 1981, p. 49.

2. *Ibid,* p. 52.

3. *Ibid,* pp. 50, 51.

4. U.S. Department of Labor, Women's Bureau, *Earnings Gap Between Women and Men* (1979), p. 2; or see L. Howe, *Pink Collar Workers,* Chapter 3.

5. B. Wertheimer, *We Were There,* p. 159.

6. G. Lapidus, "Occupational Segregation and Public Policy: A Comparative Analysis of American and Soviet Patterns," *in* M. Blaxall and B. Reagan, *Women and the Workplace,* p. 124.

7. B. and E. Reubens, "Women Workers, Nontraditional Occupations and Full Employment," in *American Women Workers in a Full Employment Economy* (Joint Economic Committee, U.S. Congress, 1977), p. 108.

8. "Women Managers Get Paid Far Less Than Males, Despite Career Gains," *Wall Street Journal* 10/7/80.

9. "Women Trained to Gain Trust of Male Bosses," *Wall Street Journal 1/16/81.*

10. "Women's Jobless Rate Drops Below Men's—Disproving an Axiom," *Wall Street Journal* 11/5/80.

Household Work

From our survey of women's labor force participation, it is clear that housework is a rather fundamental aspect of women's work. Even in the simplistic household decision-making models, someone's labor, typically the wife's, *had* to be allocated to housework. When we turned to wages, we found the speculation that women's market wages were related to women's alternate productivity in housework. In the occupational segregation literature, we noticed some analysts assuming that women duplicate in the labor market the kind of work they do in the house, as given by the "office wife" example. Furthermore, if we think of the millions of women who do housework in America, we begin to realize that this is a very important sector of women's work activity. Not only is this a type of work done by almost all women, but it is an odd sort of work in terms of our modern, cash-oriented economy: it is unpaid work that remains private. Nor are there any real standards of quality or quantity for the output of housework.

To begin to understand the peculiar character of housework, we first need to identify what housework *is,* that is, what types of labor are performed in housework. We can then focus on the central questions of why this labor is so necessary to our economy and why it is really productive work and not just "busy work" for lonely wives. Once we have an idea of the essential function of housework, we can examine it like any other work process to see how much time the different tasks require and what this type of labor is worth. We can also try to determine how this work has changed over time, if at all, and why. Ultimately, we can reach some conclusions about the effect of housework on women's other work roles, and what may need to be changed in housework if women's status in society is to improve.

What Is Housework?

Our first task is to specify what we mean by housework. It is not just puttering around the house. Neither is it some mysterious feminine role, as is implied by the term "homemaking." It is a whole work process, composed of many different tasks performed in different quantities, usually depending on the physical layout of the house and the number of people in the house. Look at Table 6-1, a summary of some recent research on time spent in housework by women and men in upstate New York.

Housework tasks include production of food, upkeep of the house and family members, and shopping and financial management. Note that women without labor market employment do the most housework (8 hours/day), followed by women with labor market jobs (5.3 hours/day), and that men do very little housework (1.6 hours/day). Although we will explore this further later on, it is important to note from the outset that most housework is done by women, not by men. Similarly, we consider all these tasks "work," even if some people say they enjoy their cooking or shopping. When some workers say they enjoy their paid jobs in the labor market, we still consider their jobs as work.

TABLE 6-1
Daily Hours Spent on Household Work

	Men	Women Employed	Not Employed
All food activities	.2	1.6	2.3
Care of the house	.6	1.2	1.6
Care of clothing	—[a]	.9	1.3
Care of family members	.4	.8	1.8
Marketing and record keeping	.4	.8	1.0
Total	1.6	5.3	8.0

[a]Less than .05 hours/day

Source: K. Walker and M. Woods, *Time Use: A Measure of Household Production of Family Goods and Services,* 1976, Washington, D.C.: American Home Economics Association (p. 50–51, 62), survey data, c. 1968.

Why Is Housework Productive and Necessary to Our Economy?

First, housework is necessary for the day-to-day operation of the economy. Without housework—the housing, feeding, clothing, and servicing of the work force—the economy would be at a standstill. Housework makes it possible for people to go to their jobs each day prepared to work. It may seem curious that such socially necessary labor goes unpaid. Later we shall see what it would cost employers if they had to pay for the value of housework performed, the true cost of preparing their workers for work. Employers would rather not absorb these costs. So it is very much in business' interest to ensure that housework be viewed as women's *role,* rather than being considered the work necessary to prepare workers for their jobs.

But housework does more than just prepare workers for their day-to-day jobs. By the way it is organized, housework also organizes our social relations. This is a complex issue, fundamentally tied to the private nature of our housework process. The very *tools* of housework have been designed to be used privately, rather than to be shared by many. Design experts have found, for instance, that our lawn mowers, vacuum cleaners, and other basic tools are too flimsy and too prone to breakdown for communal use; they require too much upkeep for neighborly sharing.[1]

The private character of housework, reinforced by the design of the equipment for private use, is essential to the organization of *consumption* on a private basis in our society. *Business Week* has warned of the consequences of any breakdown in this private consumption system:

> ... *togetherness automatically tends to reduce consumer spending; only one refrigerator is needed instead of two, one vacuum cleaner, one washing machine. Even sales of automobiles and television sets are affected.*[2]

Separate households, with their own private sets of tools and equipment, ensure higher sales for business. In fact, market forecasters watch the size and composition of our private households carefully, knowing there is a clear relationship between our social relations and our consumption of household appliances. As the *Wall Street Journal* pointed out, for example:

Magic Chef, Inc. is stressing production of microwave ovens partly because of the numbers of divorced people and singles who are setting up homes.[3]

If businesses market their products carefully, more private households mean more product sales; privatized housework remains fundamental.

On a more subtle level, a private housework system shapes our social relations in other ways. The private household is supposed to serve as a counterbalance to alienated work in the public sphere. Consider this excerpt from a leading home economics textbook:

Those who have realized how character is formed will fully grasp the importance of the woman's position in her home, in the midst of her family. The greatest task of any woman is to render as agreeable and as fruitful as possible the actual time that the other members of the family pass in the home. . . .[4]

These sentiments were echoed in a recent journal for educators:

There is a strong relationship between the sphere of the home and the sphere of the workplace, and, therefore, a powerful confluence exists between domestic stability and industrial productivity. When individuals feel isolated and experience a breakdown of the human support system to which they are accustomed, it is veritably impossible for them to function effectively and productively in their jobs.[5]

By claiming breakdowns in the home cause declines in workplace productivity, the author of this article emphasizes the strategic function the private household is supposed to have in our society. While our ideology stresses the home as refuge, reality suggests that this is not necessarily true anymore. Mental health experts have noted that the rise in child abuse, wife abuse, and rape is related to economic problems, particularly "insufficient income."[6] Even the private home may no longer be able to contain social tension.

The private home with its private housework may be essential to the maintenance of our entire economic system, then, as both a cheap method of preparing workers for their jobs and a reinforcement of our social relations structure. Private households are supposed to keep sales of consumer products buoyant, as they keep worker morale buoyant.

How Much Housework Is Done These Days?

While many people would agree that housework is necessary and productive work, few realize how much housework is actually being done. "Gross housework product" is not included in our national income account, the GNP, nor is it discussed by many social scientists. Fortunately, though, some researchers have been investigating the amount of time spent on housework, which provides us with some useful information.

Most studies of housework time are based on random samples of households in a selected area. Participants in these surveys are asked to keep a time diary, recording every activity of their working day, or they are interviewed as to how much time they spend on housework activities specifically. Results of the different surveys therefore differ according to the method of the study; they also vary with the definitions of the various tasks. One of the trickiest problems in these surveys is that different housework tasks may be performed simultaneously—for instance, stirring the soup while thinking about a shopping list. Even if the respondent remembers that she was thinking about her marketing chores and tells the interviewer, how should the researcher categorize the time spent on these two tasks? Was it cooking or budgeting work?

Obviously, the study of housework time involves some heroic assumptions, as in most social science research. But once the researcher can specify the average time spent on various housework tasks, the data can be used in a variety of ways. For example, it can help to determine the "dollar value" of housework, or a hypothetical wage. There are two basic methods by which this is done. Some economists use the *opportunity cost* approach; they reason that a woman's housework must be worth at least what she would earn if she worked in the labor market. In other words, the opportunity cost of her time in housework is what she would earn if instead she worked in a paid job. This opportunity-cost pricing method seems unsatisfactory to many housework researchers, however, because it does not reflect anything about the types of tasks done in housework.

The second approach, favored by housework time analysts, is the *replacement cost method*. It is calculated by cumulating the amount you would have to pay to hire a replacement person to do each housework task for the specified amount of time each day. If, for example, 2 hours/day are spent on cooking, and cooks usually earn $5.00/hour, and 2 hours/day are spent cleaning, and cleaners earn

$3.00/hour, those 4 hours of housework would be valued at their replacement cost, or $16.00. In Table 6-2 the results of this type of approach are shown, weighted with 1971 wage rates. According to the data, a woman's housework could be worth up to $9,400 per year in 1971 wages, which converts to $15,000 in 1980 wages. This value would differ, of course, for each particular household depending on the number and ages of children, the employment status of the wife, and the types of housework performed.

The calculations become even more significant when they are actually applied to real life situations. Insurance companies, for instance, use these types of computations to determine the value of a housewife when compensating a husband for the death of his insured wife. Recently, they have been warning policyholders to buy extra life insurance to cover the value of the housewife's unpaid labor. More controversially, women have been trying to reclaim the value of their housework services in divorce settlements, which has provoked heated court arguments about whether housework is a woman's natural function, or whether it is work.

Once most people recover from the shock of hearing that housework can be worth as much as $15,000 per year, their typical reaction is to argue that it is a "thing of the past." According to the popular advertisements, after all, labor-saving devices have reduced housework to an insignificant, minimal effort. They imply that it is not even work anymore, but more like a creative hobby. Microwave ovens cook your meals in minutes. With a food processor, you can be a gourmet chef, creating pâtés in your leisure time. We are told that the industrial revolution in the home has freed women from the drudgery of housework. But is it true?

Has the Time Spent on Housework Declined in Recent Years?

To answer this question, examine Figure 6-1, which summarizes the evidence on the average amounts of time women have spent on housework in the United States since the 1920s. All rumors to the contrary, the amount of time spent on housework has not declined, even with all our modern "labor-saving" equipment. To unravel this paradox, it will be useful to examine some of the statistical research on housework time.

Using the data from the housework time surveys, researchers have tried to find out what determines the quantity of housework

TABLE 6-2
Average Annual Dollar Value of Time Contributed by Various Family Members in all Household Work
(All Values Expressed to Nearest $100)

Number of Children	Age of Wife or Youngest Child	Value of Time Contributed in Nonemployed-Wife Households			Value of Time Contributed in Employed-Wife Households		
		Wife	Wife	Husband	Child 12–17[1]	Wife	Husband	Child 12–17[1]
0	Under 25	$3,900	$ 700	—	$2,600	$1,100	—
	25–39	4,500	900	—	2,800	1,100	—
	40–54	4,600	1,200	—	3,200	600	—
	55 and over	4,100	1,600	—	3,200	900	—
	Youngest Child						
1	12–17	$5,300	$1,600	$ 900	$3,700	$1,400	$ 800
	6–11	5,200	1,200	—	4,400	900	—
	2–5	5,200	1,400	—	3,600	1,200	—
	1	5,900	1,400	—	5,000	400	—
	under 1	6,600	1,300	—	(2)	(2)	—
2	12–17	5,600	1,300	700	3,600	1,300	900
	6–11	5,600	1,300	600	4,100	1,200	700
	2–5	6,400	1,300	600	4,800	1,400	900
	1	6,900	1,300	(3)	4,900	2,800	(3)
	under 1	7,600	1,200	(3)	6,200	1,300	(3)
3	12–17	5,000	800	800	2,800	1,200	800
	6–11	5,600	1,300	900	4,800	1,200	1,000
	2–5	6,200	1,100	900	5,900	1,700	(3)
	1	6,900	1,300	1,200	5,800	2,000	(3)
	under 1	8,000	1,200	(3)	5,200	1,700	(3)
4	12–17	4,700	800	700	4,600	1,000	1,000
	6–11	6,100	1,100	800	4,100	700	600
	2–5	7,000	1,200	600	(2)	(2)	(3)
	1	6,800	1,500	800	(2)	(2)	(3)
	under 1	8,400	1,700	(3)	(2)	(2)	(3)
5–6	6–11	6,600	1,600	1,100	(2)	(2)	(3)
	2–5	6,900	1,200	800	(2)	(2)	(3)
	1	5,800	900	(3)	(2)	(2)	(3)
	under 1	8,100	1,700	900	(2)	(2)	(3)
7–9	2–5	6,800	1,800	900	(2)	(2)	(3)
	under 1	9,400	1,500	(3)	—	—	—

[1]Values for children are for each child in the family.
[2]Fewer than 4 families.
[3]Fewer than 4 children of designated ages.

Source: Data collected by N.Y. State College of Human Ecology, Cornell University: included 1,318 urban-suburban households, Syracuse, N.Y., 1967–68, and 60 rural households, Cortland County, N.Y., 1971. Based on 1971 wage rates. K. Walker and W. Gauger, "Time and Its Dollar Value in Housework" in *Family Economics Review,* Fall 1973, p. 12.

FIGURE 6-1
Hours Per Week Devoted to Household Work

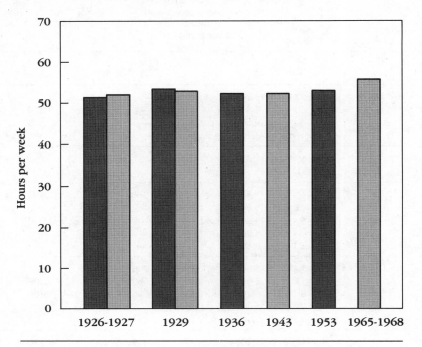

Source: J. Vanek, "Time Spent in Housework," *Scientific American,* November 1974, p. 118.

done in various homes. They have investigated, for example, whether there is a correlation between doing lower amounts of housework and being a college-educated person, or being an employee in the labor market, and so on. They have concluded that among women, the following factors are associated with lower amounts of housework, on the average: having a college education, being young (particularly 18–29 years old), being employed, being a student, not being married, having no children or few children, and employing a full-time household worker.[7] Male participation in housework is relatively independent of these factors, not increasing significantly with more children in the family and only increasing marginally (10%) if the wife is employed in the labor market.[8] In fact, researchers comment:

Those few wives whose husbands were unemployed reported higher-than-average housework.[9]

Housework time analysts also conclude from their studies that women in America have experienced a rather minor decline in housework time in recent years, an average of 22 minutes/day less from 1965 to 1975.[10] They attribute this to demographic factors rather than to technological factors. Since employed women and women with fewer children spend less time on housework, and since the number of such women has increased relative to women who are not employed or women with many children, we have experienced this slight decline, on the average, of housework time.

What about those technological factors, those "labor-saving" devices? First of all, American women spend about as much time on housework as women do in other countries *without* labor-saving devices. International housework comparisons (Table 6-3) suggest that private household access to labor-saving equipment is not really very important for reducing housework time. For example, note that people in Kazanlik, Bulgaria, spend less time on housework than we do. The reason for this appears to be that in Kazanlik, more housework services are provided on a social basis, such as communal eating facilities. Thus, it is not just the available equipment that determines housework time, but also how it is used.

TABLE 6-3
Average Amount of Time Spent on Housework
(Daily Average per Person, Including Weekends)

	Kazanlik (Bulgaria)		Pskov (USSR)		Olomouc (Czecho-slovakia)		Kragujevac (Yugo-slavia)		Jackson (USA)		Oshabrück (FRG)	
	hr	%	hr	%	hr	%	hr	%	hr	%	hr	%
Food preparation	0.6	23.0	0.9	29.0	1.1	28.2	1.1	29.8	0.7	21.9	0.8	21.0
Cleaning	0.6	23.0	0.6	19.4	0.9	23.0	0.8	21.6	0.9	28.1	1.2	31.6
Washing and ironing	0.2	8.0	0.4	12.9	0.5	12.8	0.5	13.5	0.4	12.5	0.4	10.5
Other	0.3	11.5	0.3	9.7	0.4	10.3	0.4	10.8	0.3	9.4	0.3	7.9
Garden animals	0.3	11.5	0.1	3.2	0.1	2.6	0.1	2.7	0.0	0.0	0.3	7.9
Children	0.3	11.5	0.4	12.9	0.4	10.3	0.3	8.1	0.4	12.5	0.3	7.9
Shopping errands	0.3	11.5	0.4	12.9	0.5	12.8	0.5	13.5	0.5	15.6	0.5	3.8
Total	2.6	100	3.1	100	3.9	100	3.7	100	3.2	100	3.8	100

Note: The table is based on the time budgets of all the grownup population, aged from 18–65, who were active, who lived in a working family, and who were in different branches of the industry and services of the city, but not in agricultural production.

Source: A. Szalai, *Uses of Time: Daily Activities of Urban and Suburban Populations in Twelve Countries,* p. 470.

Why Buy Labor-Saving Devices if They Do Not Save Labor?

Why? Perhaps these devices make housework tasks more pleasant. Researchers have found, however, that housewives with new equipment have similar attitudes to their tasks as those without the tools. Owning a dishwasher, iron, or dryer, for instance, did not significantly change a woman's attitude to dishwashing or laundry work, according to a recent Indiana survey. Interestingly, families with dishwashers served more meals, although the cleanup time per meal did decrease from 5.9 minutes to 5.5 minutes with a dishwasher.[11] Also, as the data in Table 6-4 indicate, households with more food preparation equipment spent more time on meal preparation than households without equipment.

The Indiana survey suggests that attitude toward a housework task, ownership of equipment, and time spent on the task are indeed related, but not in the way we would expect. As the researcher remarked with respect to laundry work:

> *The least amount of time was given to ironing by homemakers who disliked the task and had little equipment.*[12]

Since household equipment does not save time or improve the attitude toward the task, its only possible *raison d'être* is "better quality output," such as whiter sheets or better cakes. Unfortunately, there is

TABLE 6-4
Meal Preparation Time by Ownership of Equipment

Equipment	Percentage Owners	Equipment Owned		Equipment Not Owned	
		Minutes/ Meal	Hours/ Week	Minutes/ Meal	Hours/ Weeks
Mixer	98	8	10.3	7	9.6
Electric skillet	68	9	9.9	8	11.0
Pressure saucepan	41	8	10.6	8	10.0
Freezer	81	9	10.5	8	9.1
Dishwasher	20	8	10.7	9	10.1

Source: S. Manning, "Time Use in Household Tasks by Indiana Families," Purdue University Research Bulletin #837, January 1968, p. 9.

no real standard of quality for household output that researchers can measure. Furthermore, there are indications that a kind of vicious cycle of rising expectations has led to rising standards of housework quality. Before the introduction of the automatic washer, for example, people were as satisfied wearing dirtier clothes as they are now with their washer-cleaned clothes. Has the new equipment raised our expectations, our standards of cleanliness? A *Ladies Home Journal* writer explained, in the 1930s:

> *Because we housewives of today have the tools to reach it, we dig every day after the dust that grandmother left to a spring cataclysm. If few of us have nine children for a weekly bath, we have two or three for a daily immersion. If our consciences don't prick us over vacant pie shelves or empty cookie jars, they do over meals in which a vitamin may be omitted or a calorie lacking.*[13]

The discovery of germs as a source of disease gave rise to an inordinate amount of housework. Dr. Stewart Ewen describes Lysol's 1926 advertisements quite precisely:

> *Lysol divided the household into an assemblage of minutely defined dangers, so mothers were told that they should be aware that even "the doorknobs threaten (children) ... with disease.*[14]

Advertisers played up the dangers of germs in an effort to encourage housewives to buy their products and equipment. They harped on the guilt that women should feel if they had not policed their homes from the inevitable invasion of germs.

Modern manufacturers have explored new methods of selling their housework equipment. An ingenious variation on the labor-saving idea has been proposed to help sell more microwave ovens. With so many convenience foods already available for the conventional stove, who would want to invest in a microwave oven to save time? Pillsbury's vice-president for business development explains:

> *We believe microwave ovens can redefine what we mean by convenience foods.*[15]

(He was referring to their "one-minute pancakes" and "three-minute popcorn.") To sell the microwave oven, business wants to redefine the "fastness" of fast food. As a Swanson foods executive explained:

> *Take the frozen breakfast. ... Twenty minutes in a regular oven is too long. Most people would rather skip the meal altogether. As for snacks, you should be able to make them during station breaks between television programs.*[16]

The labor-saving equipment of the future may be even more grim, since the U.S. government has tried to mandate that household appliances conform to energy efficiency standards. So our appliance industry has responded with their own threat: future appliances will work less effectively:

> *Washers aren't going to clean very well, and dryers will take longer. But the microwave oven may talk and correct recipe errors, and most major appliances will diagnose their own ills.*[17]

In the future, we may return to longer and longer hours of housework, just to get the clothes as clean as we are used to today (but our ovens may chat with us to help the time go by).

While the American experience with labor-saving devices has not been encouraging, there are exceptions. Much depends on how the technology is actually employed. As we saw in Table 6-1, labor-market employed women spend less time on their housework than do full-time housewives. Perhaps they accomplish less, but they also seem to work in a time-efficient manner with their equipment.[18] It is not necessarily the equipment that matters, as much as *how* the equipment is used. With a severe time constraint, some employed women *can* use these tools to perform their housework more quickly.

With this rather dismal verdict on labor-saving equipment in the home, we return to our basic analysis of the role of housework in the economy, mindful that housework still takes a great deal of time. In fact, all indications point to more time being spent on housework in our present economy. Why? Because inflation has recently become a more permanent feature of our developed economy, and inflation means more housework.

The Inflation of Housework

Even if household income *could* keep pace with inflation, rapidly and unevenly rising consumer prices mean more time has to be spent managing consumption: keeping track of relative prices, switching buying strategies, and shopping aggressively. Furthermore, since household income does not keep pace with inflation, most housewives have to compensate for their decline in purchasing power by doing more housework. This can mean a return to producing more goods in the home "from scratch" and perhaps starting a garden to grow certain foods, using coupons to save money, sewing rather than buying most clothing, and so forth. Inflation means more housework for everyone.[19]

In addition, the need for more purchasing power pushes more women into the labor force. Thus inflation may require more housework and more waged work too. These double jobs are the classic "double burden" of women, and their prevalence seems to be on the increase. The price women pay is enormous. As noted earlier, employed women still get very little assistance from other family members in performing housework. They end up reducing their sleeping time and their leisure time to a minimum. Furthermore, research indicates that this stress leads women to the unhealthy use of various tranquilizers, which barely masks an intolerable work burden.[20]

What can be done? What could reduce women's burdens? One remedy is obvious. Men could share the housework more equitably. This would certainly reduce women's workload, and it might also reduce the total amount of desired housework to be performed. While marketing experts have begun to explore the tastes of the male shopper, the phenomenon is still quite limited. It is expected to increase, however, since delayed marriages and high divorce rates mean more single men in the population.[21]

Rather than just wait for the men to share the work, some women have gone a step further by organizing "wages for housework" campaigns. The logic of this is simple. Housework, like all other work in our society, should be financially compensated. This is not only just, but would probably elevate social consciousness of the necessity of this work. It might also lead us to question how inefficiently we have organized the provision of housework services. After all, as pointed out earlier, wages for housework would be substantial as housework is presently organized. If our economy actually had to pay the cost of those wages, there might be more interest in restructuring housework, which would be a first step in lifting women's double burden.

While utopians throughout the ages have proposed ingenious solutions for the problem of housework, we may not need to look to science fiction for our solutions. Surveys of housework time indicate that students spend very little time on housework, compared to other people. Perhaps the experts should examine student life a bit more closely. Think about those dormitories with linen services and dining halls—some even with professional cleaning services. Couldn't apartment buildings and neighborhoods have similar services available?

Additional Readings

For the history of housework in America, a good place to start is Part VI, "Mechanization Encounters the Household," of S. Giedion's *Mechanization Takes Command* (Norton, 1948). This could be followed up with Joann Vanek's "Housewives as Workers" *in* A. Stromberg and S. Harkess, *Women Working* (Mayfield, 1978). For a more political perspective on the housework question, see B. Weinbaum and A. Bridges, "The Other Side of the Paycheck," *in* Z. Eisenstein, ed., *Capitalist Patriarchy and the Case for Socialist Feminism* (Monthly Review, 1979). For a more theoretical perspective on the history of housework, see B. Berch, "The Development of Housework," *International Journal of Women's Studies,* Vol. 1, no. 4, 1978. If you are interested in estimates of time spent on housework (and other work) worldwide, consult the encyclopedia of time-use studies, A. Szalai, ed., *The Uses of Time: Daily Activities of Urban and Suburban Populations in Twelve Countries* (The Hague, Mouton, 1972).

Notes

1. V. Papanek and J. Hennessey, *How Things Don't Work,* Chapter 2.
2. "Economic Diary, Nov. 21, 1980: Vanishing Households: A Drag on the Economy," *Business Week* 12/8/80.
3. "Household Growth Could Spurt in '80s, But Much Hinges on Lifestyle Choices," *Wall Street Journal* 7/1/80.
4. Quoted in J. Bane and M. Chapin, *Introduction to Home Economics,* p. 111.
5. L. Gurtin, "The Benefits of Family Stability," *Collegiate Forum,* Fall 1980.
6. "Over the Brink: Inflation Can Ruin Mental Health, Therapists Believe," *Wall Street Journal* 5/15/80.
7. J. Robinson, *How Americans Use Time,* pp. 66, 67.
8. *Ibid,* p. 68.
9. *Ibid,* p. 69.
10. K. Newland, *Women, Men and the Division of Labor,* p. 22.
11. S. Manning, "Time Use in Household Tasks by Indiana Families," Purdue University Research Bulletin #837, January 1968, pp. 12, 26.
12. *Ibid,* p. 26.
13. Ehrenreich and English, "The Manufacture of Housework," *Socialist Revolution* 26, Vol. 5 #4 Oct./Dec. 1975, pp. 7, 8.
14. S. Ewen, *Captains of Consciousness,* p. 170.
15. "Will New Foods Help the Market for Ovens?" *Business Week* 7/31/78.
16. "Microwave Ovens Gaining," *New York Times* 12/6/79.
17. "Proposed Energy Rules Promise New Breed of Major Appliances," *Wall Street Journal* 12/10/80. (For better or for worse, the Reagan administration decided to cancel these guidelines.)
18. For a discussion of this time-efficient mode of housework, see B. Berch, "The Development of Housework," *International Journal of Women's Studies,* Vol. 1, no. 4, pp. 336–348, 1978.

19. For further elaboration, see B. Berch, "The Inflation of Housework" in *Brooklyn College Monograph Series,* 1981.

20. See, for example, "Steep Inflation Means Cutbacks in Essentials for Poorest Families," *Wall Street Journal* 3/27/80. (All the women interviewed by the *Journal* for this article were given Valium or Darvon by their doctors to help them cope with the stress caused by their financial pressures.)

21. See, for example, "More Food Advertisers Woo the Male Shopper as He Shares the Load," *Wall Street Journal* 8/26/80, or, "More Working Wives Expose Their Hubbies to the Joy of Cooking," *Wall Street Journal* 10/16/80.

7

Childbearing Work

Few people are willing to look at childbearing as "work." To label it an "economically productive activity" is even more awkward; it suggests a functional, almost eugenic approach that makes us uncomfortable. It seems to deny the emotional, humanistic side of childbearing. Without debating the aesthetic appeal of babies, however, we need to address ourselves to the *other* side of childbearing, which exists even if we try to ignore it. Bearing and raising children is economically productive labor that women perform for society. It is nothing less than the production of the future labor force, without which our economy could not endure.

While as individuals we may view childbearing as an intensely personal activity, we must also recognize that because it is vital for the economy, it is also structured by our economic system in a very deliberate fashion. We have laws prohibiting certain types of sexual intercourse, laws prohibiting women from terminating their own pregnancies, laws to give tax incentives for having children, and so forth. Our government indirectly controls the quantity of children that women produce. They define which costs will be paid by the private parents and which will be paid by the state. So, far from being a purely emotional and personal issue, childbearing is also a very public economic question. Furthermore, on the individual level, the decision to bear children affects a woman's lifetime earnings profile more than anything else. It is vitally important, then, to set aside emotional concerns for the moment and to focus on the economic dimensions of childbearing.

109

The Economic Model of Fertility: The Cost-Benefit Approach

What are these "economic dimensions" of childbearing? As a starting point, we can examine the economists' models of fertility behavior; again, even if they are not useful, their shortcomings are instructive. For modern economists, fertility is another rational choice problem. Childbearing can yield two types of benefits: the pleasure that children give their parents (the *consumer durables* model) and the insurance against indigent old age (the *producer durables* model). Childbearing also involves two types of costs: time and money. Rational couples weigh the costs against the benefits, and choose to have the optimal number of children. (The net returns from an additional child must be greater than the net returns from any alternative use of their time and income.) Then they select time- or money-intensive childbearing methods, depending on the relative costs of time and money for the particular family. Parents who are rich, or whose time is highly paid, can use money-intensive child-rearing techniques: fancy toys and expensive childcare. Poor or low-wage parents can use time-intensive methods: reading stories or playing games with their children.

Although this model is certainly interesting, is it realistic? By identifying the shortcomings of these economistic models, we begin to realize what the *real* variables are. One basic problem with the models is that they assume that fertility decisions are a matter of choice. Are they? Contraceptive information is not universal, nor is infertility universally curable. According to contemporary estimates, one of every five couples in America is infertile.[1] Even when choice *is* possible, it may be wrong to assume that *collective* choice decisions are possible; the costs and benefits of childbearing are very different for the man and the woman, as maternal mortality statistics indicate. In the United States, more women die from childbirth than from legal abortion. Recent statistics indicate that "for white women the risk of death from childbirth ... is almost twenty times as great as the risk of death from legal abortion."[2] Thus, the potential hazard to a woman's health does indeed make truly collective childbirth decisions rather difficult. Not only do husband and wife run different risks in the decision, but in the long run the wife will probably assume a much greater burden of childcare responsibilities, as our time-use studies indicate.

Even if a couple can make a meaningful collective fertility decision, their private calculation of costs and benefits may be completely overshadowed by societal constraints. The economists' fertility models assume that choice is a very private affair, but in reality certain government policies may influence these decisions. While European and third-world families are used to explicit national population policies, they seem somewhat shocking to average Americans. American government population policies are generally quite subtle. We do not have family allowances or subsidies to large families for basic food and transportation costs; nonetheless, we *do* have a fertility policy.

American Population Policy

As we observed in Chapter 2, America has been a labor-scarce country since colonial times, and our government policy has been pro-natal to counteract this scarcity. A good example of this is our labor legislation covering women workers. This legislation was *not* designed to help women workers earn a decent living or to protect women from discrimination. It was passed (and judged constitutional) only because by protecting women workers, it protected the unborn generations of workers these women would bear. In the famous 1908 *Muller v. Oregon* case, which tested the legality of protective legislation for women, the argument was stated quite frankly: "... as healthy mothers are essential to vigorous offspring, the physical well-being of women becomes an object of public interest and care in order to preserve the strength and vigor of the race."[3] Just as protective legislation was supposed to protect women's capacity to bear children, other legislation has forced women actually to bear these children: legislation prohibiting contraceptives and abortion.[4]

While most people assume these laws are purely moralistic, their economic function is also quite real. When abortions are illegal, for instance, more women stay out of the labor force to bear children, which shrinks the unemployment rate *and* ensures a generous supply of workers in the future. While the positive incentives to bear children are weak in the United States relative to some European countries, our tax system *does* reward childbearers with tax exemptions. In the armed forces, childbearing families are rewarded with larger housing facilities, another type of positive incentive.

The only real exceptions to the overall pro-natalism of U.S. policy are our sterilization programs, where often economically or socially "undesirable" mothers are unwittingly sterilized by medical officials. It has been estimated that 35% of all women of childbearing age in

Puerto Rico and up to 25% of all Native American women have been sterilized.[5] Noting the prevalence of sterilization operations among low-income or non-white women, health activists have worked recently for guidelines covering these procedures. Overall, a wide range of U.S. legislation—labor law, abortion law, and tax law—is related to a desire (either conscious or unconscious) to control women's childbearing activity in the interests of the state.

Who Pays the Costs of Childbearing?

Ironically, even though the government sees women as the mothers of the future labor supply and tries to direct their childbearing decisions, it is individual women (or couples) who pay the costs of this childbearing. Like housework, childbearing is economically productive, necessary work that is performed by women and unpaid. It is not only unpaid, but very expensive. In 1980 the direct monetary cost of bearing and raising a child for a middle-class family averaged $85,088. These costs are detailed in Table 7-1.

TABLE 7-1
Direct Costs of Raising a Child (in 1980)

Childbirth	$ 2,485
Housing	24,711
Food	17,931
Transport	12,027
Clothes	5,686
Medical	3,718
Educational materials	1,020
Four-year (state) college	9,784
Other	7,726
Total	$85,088

Source: "Costs of Being a Parent Keep Going Higher," *Wall Street Journal* 10/3/80.

While the estimates may seem high, they have increased in recent years only at a rate comparable to the rate of inflation (that is, during the three-year period from 1977 to 1980 they have gone up 33%, on the average). Some cost components, such as childbirth costs, may increase sharply, with the growth of "high-tech" birthing (fetal monitors, caesarean births, and so forth).

The direct costs of bearing and raising a child are low compared to the indirect costs borne by the mother herself. These indirect costs are usually termed "opportunity costs" by the economists; in this case they are the wages the mother would have earned had she remained in (or entered) the labor force. Two-thirds of the mothers of young children in America are not in the labor force. Why? For low-waged women, the cost of child care might easily absorb most of their net earnings if they kept working.

While economists have traditionally measured opportunity costs of this type in a straightforward manner, multiplying the absent time by the wage rate (for example, 3 years at $12,000/year = $36,000 in foregone earnings), they have begun to re-think this entire calculation. They have discovered that when a mother returns to full-time employment, she can rarely compensate for her absence from the work force. This can be illustrated simply with "age-earnings" profiles, as in Figure 7-1.

The age-earnings profile shows the level of earnings a person might receive at each age, over the course of their lifetime. The upper profile, for instance, could represent an average woman with no children, who starts her first job at age 20 at $10,000/year and who stays in the labor force until retirement. Her salary increases continually until age 35, when it levels off at a steady $35,000/year. The second profile might illustrate the age-earnings path of a woman who leaves the labor force at age 25 to have children. She "breaks" her earnings here for five years and then returns to the labor force.

FIGURE 7-1
Age–Earnings Profiles

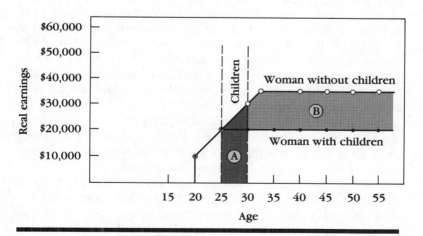

Traditionally, only shaded area *A* was considered foregone earnings; this is what the woman would have earned during those five years. Now economists are looking at shaded area *B* as well, since they have found that the lifetime earnings profiles of mothers in the labor force never seem to "catch up" with earnings profiles of non-mothers or, of course, of men. The reasons for this depend on the age of the mother. Early childbearing may interrupt the woman's schooling, permanently lowering her earnings capacity. This is particularly critical now, in light of the current explosion of teenage mothers (in 1976, teenage mothers were responsible for one out of every five births in the United States). If a woman finishes her schooling and then leaves the labor force for childbearing, she leaves her career during its optimal growth phase. But if a woman postpones childbearing until her career is well established, she may pay dearly for that extra time in the labor force, since medical authorities warn of the hazards of late childbearing.

Whether they have children early or late, bunched or spaced, most mothers pay the medical and financial costs of childbearing themselves. If a mother leaves the labor force to care for her child, this usually means there is less family income at precisely the time when expenses have risen sharply. One way some women cope with this income loss is by taking in foster children, since the government pays a fee to the foster family for each such child. While this fee is by no means large, it can supplement family income when the mother is staying out of the labor market to take care of her own children. Currently, about 67% of all children in "care" are in foster homes, compared to 13% in legal adoption homes.[6]

If the mother does not leave the labor force to care for her child, but cannot afford day care, she may try shiftwork, that is, a night job. If she can arrange for her husband or a relative to care for the child in the evening, she can take a paid job for the night hours and care for the child herself in the daytime. However, most women's night jobs (waitressing and nursing, for example) do not pay the premium wages many men's night jobs command. Low wages, exhaustion, and stress make the shiftwork-at-night/child-care-by-day formula relatively difficult for women to manage.

A few mothers, particularly those in well-paid occupations, keep their jobs and arrange professional day care for their children. Many other mothers may keep their jobs and set up free or very low-cost daycare involving informal arrangements with relatives of the family. But mothers without these low-cost options may have to pay more than they can afford. As one expert concluded, "It is apparent that the daily salary of at least half of working women did not provide the cost of a single child's day care meeting federal standards."[7] It is interesting that when business was desperate for women workers during World War II, they set up nurseries right in the factories, recognizing that women needed these arrangements for their children in order to work. Under peacetime conditions, with a full supply of labor in the market, business feels no incentive to share the costs of raising the future labor supply, and the burden falls back on the mothers.

Knowledge of this burden has certainly been a key factor in the current trend in the United States toward a lower birth rate, although some social critics tend to blame the women's liberation movement for our declining birth rates. Overall, the modern women's movement has been remarkably pro-natal, fighting for women's rights to a family *and* a job. It is more likely that access to contraception and increased knowledge of the true costs of childbearing have kept women from having unwanted children.

Some Implications of a Declining Birth Rate

Market analysts have been eyeing our declining birth rates anxiously, since a low birth rate may mean they have "too few mouths to feed," or in other words, a shrinking domestic sales market in the future. When they speak of our "baby bust" (the opposite of a "baby boom"), they are forced to contemplate the shrinkage of some traditionally robust industries—first the baby product industries and later the teen and adult markets. Yet the picture for business is not entirely bleak, since they have found that sales can remain buoyant if the baby bust generation spends more per person than earlier generations have.

As a recent study of maternity spending concluded, "The relative affluence of the older women having babies is evident in the maternity-wear stores. 'In the past you had a woman 20 to 23, who was maybe a secretary, getting pregnant,' says Peter Morrison, chief of population studies for Rand Corp. in Santa Monica. 'Now a woman is, say, 29 years old, and perhaps she's in marketing or is an attorney. She has a bigger income to spend on clothing. She also doesn't have the time to sit home and make clothes.' "[8]

Even if the lower birth rate does not hurt maternity goods sales, it does indicate a smaller labor force in America in 20 years. Some businessmen view this prospect with concern, since a labor shortage would tend to increase real wages. They see "the possibility that labor scarcity will eventually inhibit investment and spur wage inflation as fast-growing industries seek to attract workers from other jobs."[9] Neo-

Malthusian analyses of the relationship between population levels and wage levels have become popular recently, largely due to these predictions of a shrinking labor force in America.[10]

Futuristic Reproduction

Yet all these birth rate calculations may soon be completely old-fashioned. The labor force of the future may be conceived and developed in the laboratory, not in the home—with genetic preselection for "desirable traits." Science fiction may soon become scientific fact. The research has already begun.[11] It started with artificial insemination, or laboratory fertilization of women. The next step was "in vitro" fertilization ("test-tube" babies), in which eggs are fertilized outside the mother and returned to her body for a normal pregnancy period. These techniques were developed to cope with male infertility. But scientists have been developing approaches to female infertility as well. As of this writing, an unknown number of "surrogate mothers" are carrying the artificially inseminated babies of infertile wives, under agreement to give the baby to the original couple when it is born. (The infertile wife's husband donates the sperm.) While the legality of this social arrangement has been challenged (the courts interpret the paying of surrogate mothers as a form of child sale), technically it is only an artificial insemination procedure. To avoid the ultimate baby transfer from the surrogate mother, however, scientists have been working on what they call "artificial embryonation," or prenatal adoption. This involves removing the fertilized egg from the surrogate mother and transplanting it back inside the infertile wife for the remainder of the pregnancy. Scientists even envision egg banks, like sperm banks, to "store" a woman's childbearing capacity for an opportune phase in her life for pregnancy. Their underlying intentions seem far less benign. They would like to be able to fertilize and grow fetuses in the laboratory, rather than rely on women's bodies.

Ultimately, scientists want to be able to read the genetic code more precisely, to be able to preselect conceptions and determine the qualities of the future labor force. Brave new world, indeed. Legal and ethical questions aside, all these developments can be seen as a logical (and perverse) outcome of a rational market economy: women being paid to produce children for other couples or babies being engineered with their future labor force potential in mind. These developments will certainly force women, perhaps for the first time, to reassess their childbearing function. However futuristic these schemes may seem, the fact that these issues *are* discussed and researched today indicates a very real concern over women's willingness to bear and raise children. As we have seen, this willingness may not depend as much on the emotional appeal of babies as on the real economic costs that women pay if they decide to bear and raise children.

Additional Readings

One of the best brief discussions of the economics of childbearing is Chapter 15 of Jessie Bernard's *The Future of Motherhood* (Penguin, 1975), although the entire book is quite relevant. Linda Gordon's *Woman's Body, Woman's Right* (Viking, 1976) offers a theory of the history of American reproductive attitudes and practices. Peck and Senderowitz's anthology, *Pronatalism: The Myth of Mom and Apple Pie* (Crowell, 1974) has some interesting articles on the hidden dynamics of pro-natalism in America. Futuristic trends in childbearing are discussed in "New Frontiers in Conception," *New York Times Magazine,* July 20, 1980.

Notes

1. "New Frontiers in Conception," *New York Times Magazine,* July 20, 1980, p. 20.
2. Data from *Women Under Attack,* Committee for Abortion Rights and Against Sterilization Abuse (CARASA), p. 5.
3. *Muller v. Oregon,* quoted by L. Kanowitz, *Sex Roles in Law and Society* (1973), p. 47.
4. Ironically, the same parties who decry "government interference" in private affairs are the first to demand government interference in women's childbearing decisions. . . .
5. Data from *Women Under Attack,* CARASA, p. 50.
6. A. Billingsley and J. Giovanni, *Children of the Storm* (1972), p. 70.
7. S. Levitan and K. Alderman, *Child Care and ABC's Too* (1975), p. 44.
8. "Sales of Maternity Clothes are Booming, Fueled by Working Women Pregnancies," *Wall Street Journal* 7/14/80.
9. "Population Changes That Help For a While," *Business Week,* September 3, 1979, p. 184.
10. See, for instance, R. Easterlin, *Birth and Fortune* (1980), or L. Jones, *Great Expectations* (1980).
11. The source of this information is "New Frontiers in Conception," *New York Times Magazine,* July 20, 1980.

What Is the Government Doing for Women?

It has been customary to think that the government is actively engaged in improving women's economic position. Commissions study women's economic status and formulate overall economic policy and specific economic programs. The government is responsible for constructing and implementing antidiscrimination laws and for guaranteeing women equal pay for equal work and fair treatment on the job. This is reasonable, after all, since government is meant to serve the people, and women are over half of "the people."

In this chapter we will carefully examine the government's policies as they affect the economic status of women. Do government policies really affect women's economic environment? Do these policies serve women's needs? Are they formulated with women's priorities in mind? To answer these questions, we must explore the various levels of government policy to see what the government's impact on women's status has been. Government can act in three major capacities: as a lawmaker, as an economic policy maker, and as a major employer. We shall examine each in turn.

The Government as Lawmaker

First, let us examine the government's lawmaking role. Laws defining women's rights can aid individual women and women as a group, with the potential for enabling long-term social change. The impact of a single law *can* be enormous. Yet while law can be a powerful instrument, it is often the instrument of powerful agents in our society. When we examine government legislation, we must be aware of the motivation for passing the law, the courts' interpretation, and the enforcement history. Seemingly benevolent interests can promote apparently benign legislation that actually acts against women's interests, or powerfully progressive legislation can be eviscerated by judicial interpretation or lack of enforcement. Since the matter of legislation is so complex, we shall focus here on one small portion of government legislation affecting women: antidiscrimination laws.

From Protection to Equal Pay

As you may recall from Chapter 3, around the turn of the century various states passed "protective legislation" to limit the hours of women's labor in certain industries and to specify certain conditions under which women would work. Usually, night work was forbidden, and women were not allowed to lift materials of certain weights. While these were called protective laws, they effectively meant that women were barred from many jobs that men could take. Women were either forced to offer themselves at a discount to employers, in order to make it worthwhile to the employers to hire them, or they were forced into the pink-collar ghetto, which usually was not covered by legislation. Protective legislation is a classic case of laws that appear beneficial but have the opposite effect. Under the guise of helping the defenseless working woman, they actually made it more difficult for women to compete for jobs or to earn a living wage.

In the 1960s, women finally received some useful federal legislation—the Equal Pay Act of 1963. This act required that men and women doing the same work in the same establishment be paid the same wage. As you might guess, this is an easy law to evade: there are hundreds of occupational titles, so any employer who wants to discriminate against women can do it quite legally if the women are given slightly different job titles from the men. Before the Equal Pay Act was in effect, many employers maintained a female wage and a male wage for any given job, as described in a 1945 case:

> ... *GE professionally studied the jobs to determine the degree of skill, effort and responsibility involved, it reduced the wage rate by one-third if the job was being performed by women.* ...[1]

After the Equal Pay Act, maintaining a female rate and a male rate for the same job was illegal. But then:

. . . the company [GE] struck the words "female" and "male" and changed the male grades 1 through 10 . . . to 6 through 15.[2]

Women were kept in the job grades 1 through 5 and barred from grades 6 through 15. The wording of the Equal Pay Act almost seems to invite this type of evasion, since women do not have to be paid equally if their jobs are not identical. Fortunately, the courts have broadened the definition of "identical" to mean "substantially equal," but even then women have problems arguing that their work is substantially the same as some men's work.

The historical impact of sex-segregated labor markets has been to create pink-collar gettos, which include primarily women workers and a few men who do "substantially equal" work. Women in sexually mixed workplaces find bias problems in the job evaluation system itself. Industrial job evaluators seem to find "physical effort as being worth twice the value of mental effort."[3] These evaluators upgrade physical jobs disproportionately, which generally works against women.

The Civil Rights Act and Women

The Equal Pay Act covered wage discrimination only, and defined it quite narrowly. The next major step forward for women came with the provisions under Title VII of the Civil Rights Act of 1964. This prohibited discrimination in more aspects of employment (including hiring, firing, promotion, and benefits) on the basis of race, color, religion, national origin, or sex. It banned discrimination by employers, as well as by unions or employment agencies.

This legal right to equal treatment in employment seemed to contradict the old state protective laws, which treated women unequally, even if under the guise of protection. This was an issue the courts had to decide. Should women be "protected" from lifting heavy objects, for instance, or should they have the right to equal employment opportunity? The courts decided in favor of Title VII, using the following sort of argument:

Title VII rejects just this type of romantic paternalism as unduly Victorian and instead vests individual women with the power to decide whether or not to take on unromantic tasks. Men have always had the right to determine whether the incremental increase in remuneration for strenuous, dangerous, obnoxious, boring or unromantic tasks is worth the candle. The promise of Title VII is that women are now to be on an equal footing.[4]

Title VII gave women the right to equal access to jobs, unencumbered by state protective legislation.

Recently, Title VII has been used to extend the coverage of the fairly limited Equal Pay Act. As discussed, the Equal Pay Act only covers equal pay for substantially similar work; it cannot cover situations of job downgrading. In a recent case against Westinghouse, women charged that the company openly sex segregated its job classifications in the 1930s, keeping women in the lowest ranks only, where they were paid less. Then, in the 1960s, when Westinghouse merged the male and female rankings to conform to Title VII, women's jobs stayed at the bottom of the merged rankings. While the trial court dismissed the women's complaint, since it involved unequal pay for unequal work, the appeals court decided that the case fell under Title VII because:

> *Title VII prohibits an employer from paying more per hour to welders than plumbers if the reason for the employer paying higher wages to the welder is that the majority of the welders are Protestants, and that the majority of the plumbers are Catholic.* [5]

Sex pay differences would fall under the same logic and would also be discriminatory. If this decision stands, it will mean a major step forward in women's rights to equal pay for work of comparable worth, a more flexible yardstick of equality than "substantially similar" work, which is rare in a sex-segregated work force.

The Affirmative Action Mandate

Under Title VII, then, women workers have had the right to equal employment opportunities, even if it usually has required a long and difficult legal struggle to prove that rights have been denied. Realizing how difficult it is for individuals to sue for their civil rights, the government tried a very interesting approach. They decided to bind federal contractors to uphold Title VII in a *positive* way: large federal contractors would have to design affirmative action programs that would set goals for overcoming discrimination. This was the mandate of Executive Order 11246, amended by Executive Order 11375 in 1967 to include sex discrimination. Major government contractors had to analyze their own job structures to see where women and minorities were underrepresented; they were then required to write a timetable of progress for these problem areas. Specifically, they had to identify what they planned to do to meet these goals, in terms of recruiting, hiring, and training. (Thus an affirmative action program is not a set of quotas, nor a requirement that certain individuals be hired.) Under these Executive Orders, if a firm wants major government contracts, it has to file an affirmative action program with the government. In other words, all employers, unions, and employment agencies must uphold the Civil Rights Act, but firms that want large government contracts must file affirmative action programs in addition. However, a contractor is not then committed to meeting *quotas* of hiring blacks or women; the affirmative action plan requires only "good faith efforts" at compliance. Even "good faith efforts" may not be necessary under the Reagan administration, as the affirmative action principle itself has been attacked.

Has Legislation Guaranteed Progress?

While subsequent legislation has extended coverage of various acts to different categories of workers, these are the major legal instruments on the books today. We have the laws to ensure that women receive equal pay and equal employment opportunities. However, the gap between the laws and the social reality is enormous. Since 1963, for instance, women are supposed to be paid for equal work. But we know from our earnings data that the male–female earnings gap has widened. If discrimination in education was banned in 1972 and discrimination in hiring was banned in 1964, why are women's wages still so much lower than men's?

The answer is quite obvious. Making discrimination illegal does not ensure that it will not happen anymore, which is why the government is responsible for making *and* enforcing laws. The lack of government enforcement of its sex discrimination laws has been the key to their failure. The backlog of complaints is enormous, as shown in Table 8-1. If employers *are* prosecuted, the penalties are fairly minor and rarely retroactive. Sex discrimination judgments seldom include class relief payments, unlike judgments in racial discrimination cases. And many firms never bother paying the court-determined settlements to their workers (see Table 8-2).

In normal economic times, most companies have little to fear if their discriminatory practices provoke a court case. In a recessionary economy, the offending firm feels even more secure, knowing the government will be sympathetic to the firm's financial health. Everyone is wary of the Pyrrhic victory that is used as a threat if employers are found guilty of widespread discrimination and assessed large penalty costs. Bankruptcy, and the subsequent joblessness of the discriminated-against workers, is a powerful threat in economic recessions.

TABLE 8-1
Complaints Filed Against Establishments

	Total	New Coverage	Old Coverage	Complaint Backlog
Fiscal Year				
1969	385	NA	NA	NA
1970	733	NA	NA	NA
1971	1,203	NA	NA	456
1972	1,122	NA	NA	432
1973	2,095	NA	NA	1,201
1974	2,864	NA	NA	1,487
1975	2,727	375	2,352	1,790
1976	2,311	253	2,058	1,860
1976[1]	447	77	370	1,793
Sept. 21, 1976–Jan. 20, 1977	454	77	377	1,800

[1]Transition quarter, June 21–Sept. 20, 1976.

Note: Litigation—Over 1,024 cases have been filed since the effective date of the Equal Pay Act of 1963.

Source: Hearings, p. 79; M. Greenberger and D. Gutmann, "Legal Remedies Beyond Title VII to Combat Sex Discrimination in Employment," in Joint Economic Committee, Congress of the United States, 95th Congress 1st Session, *American Women Workers in a Full Employment Economy: A Compendium of Papers* (USGPO, 1977).

Not surprisingly, enforcement is generally seen as the major problem with the federal antidiscrimination legislation. This is not because enforcement is inherently difficult; rather, it is in the area of enforcement that government defers to business's interests.

Current Controversies: Pregnancy, Sexual Harassment, and Reverse Discrimination

Apart from the enforcement problem, there are a few key policy issues in equal employment law that are provoking controversy, and most involve interpretations of Title VII provisions. For instance, can school boards require pregnant school teachers to take leave without pay after the fourth or fifth month of pregnancy? The Supreme Court found this requirement illegal under the Fourteenth Amendment:

> *While the regulations requiring leave no doubt represent a good-faith attempt to achieve a laudable goal, they cannot pass muster under the Due Process of the Fourteenth Amendment, because they*

TABLE 8-2
Equal Pay Findings

Fiscal Year	Number of Employees Underpaid under the Equal Pay Act	Amount Found Due	Income Restored Employees	Income Restored Amount
1965	960	$ 156,202	NA	NA
1966	6,633	2,097,600	NA	NA
1967	5,931	3,252,319	NA	NA
1968	6,622	2,448,405	NA	NA
1969	16,100	4,585,344	NA	NA
1970	17,719	6,119,265	NA	NA
1971	29,992	14,842,994	NA	NA
1972	29,022	14,030,889	NA	NA
1973	29,619[1]	18,005,582[1]	17,331[1]	$ 4,626,251[1]
1974	32,792	20,623,830[2]	16,769[2]	6,841,443[2]
1975	31,843	26,484,860	17,889	7,474,163
1976	24,610	17,952,212	16,728	7,881,502
1976[3]	2,402	1,487,464	1,765	650,217
Sept. 21, 1976–Jan. 20, 1977	4,930	3,503,786	4,297	2,088,559
Total	239,175	$35,590,752	74,778	$29,562,135
Sept. 21, 1975–Jan. 20, 1976	9,182	$ 7,963,667	5,777	$ 3,074,046

[1]Not included in these figures is $6,300,000 paid under the Equal Pay Act by American Telephone & Telegraph to 6,100 of its employees. While the violative practice was originally disclosed by several wage-hour investigations, the resolution of the problem throughout the entire American Telephone & Telegraph operating system was secured through litigation by the Solicitor's Office but was not based on individual compliance actions. This amount is thus not included in wage-hour compliance action statistics.

[2]Not included in these figures is $7,000,000, which the company agreed to restore to 7,000 employees. This is the second consent decree which was entered into with AT&T covering equal pay violations at management level.

[3]Transition quarter, June 21–Sept. 20, 1976.

Source: Hearings, p. 83; M. Greenberger and D. Gutmann, "Legal Remedies Beyond Title VII to Combat Sex Discrimination in Employment," in Joint Economic Committee, Congress of the United States, 95th Congress 1st Session, *American Women Workers in a Full Employment Economy: A Compendium of Papers* (USGPO, 1977).

employ unrebuttable presumptions that unduly penalize a female teacher for deciding to bear a child.[6]

On the other hand, the courts decided that company insurance schemes did not have to include pregnancy with other worker disabilities, so here Congress had to pass specific legislation. Title VII, as amended, requires that pregnant women be treated the same as other employees, including being given leave or benefits for any disability. The courts may also have to clarify policy on the question of employment discrimination and reproductive hazards. Recently, OSHA (Occupational Safety and Health Administration) has tried to penalize firms for demanding that their women workers be sterilized in order to prevent possible exposure of fetuses to lead poisoning. OSHA took the position that "the company could not seek to eliminate the hazard by forcing the women to choose between losing their jobs and undergoing sterilization."[7] Ideally, a hazard-free workplace would eliminate the need for this controversy, but in the meantime sex discrimination law is being invoked for these cases.

Another key issue recently defined under the rubric of affirmative active policy has been sexual harassment on the job. The government has issued guidelines defining what constitutes harassment and prohibiting it, with the understanding that affirmative action plans can be undermined by on-site harassment of women employees.

Unfortunately, the whole affirmative action concept has been under attack by those who claim they are victims of *reverse discrimination*. Since affirmative action is only a commitment by firms to make "good faith efforts" toward eliminating the effects of past discriminatory practices, and since it includes *no* quota systems, it is difficult to imagine why white men, for instance, now feel discriminated against. They can no longer reap the benefits of a privileged status and can no longer expect to be employed on more favorable terms than women or minorities, but that hardly seems to constitute discrimination.

The Next Frontier: Comparable Worth

Probably the most important policy area to be argued in the next few years will be the issue of equal pay for work of *comparable worth*. As noted earlier, the equal pay for similar work provisions of the 1963 Equal Pay Act covers only a fairly narrow range of cases. Due to sex segregation of our labor markets, women and men do not usually *do* the same work. In many cases, women are doing comparable quality or even higher quality work for less pay than men. It is not clear at this point whether this issue can be settled under Title VII, as indicated earlier, or whether new policy will have to be formulated. What is clear is that the business community is fundamentally opposed to the concept of comparable worth. As written in *Business Week:*

> *Comparable worth may be the civil rights issue of the 1980s, and it could cost employers billions in payroll dollars.*[8]

Indeed, a business lobbying group, the Equal Employment Advisory Council, has spent many thousands of its estimated $1 million annual budget trying to fight the comparable worth idea. The cases are already in the courts; the outcomes will be quite significant for the women's pay issue.

The Government as Economic Policy Maker

While most people agree that the government is responsible for formulating a national economic policy, there is considerably less agreement on the nature of that policy. Should the government pursue specific target programs aimed at particular economic problems? This direct approach could mean, for example, economic programs aimed at eliminating sex discrimination in specific areas, such as women as small business entrepreneurs or women's access to the credit markets.

Or should the government try a more indirect approach? There are two basic indirect routes of government policy. First, the government can try to improve the functioning of the economy at large (*macroeconomic* policy) and thereby help women (by full employment spending, for instance). Alternatively, the government can aid private businesses, which in turn aid whom they wish (by hiring more women, blacks, whites, or whomever). While in recent years the government has tried a combination of direct programs and indirect macroeconomic programs, recent government endorsements of *supply-side economics* seem to indicate a shift toward the help-business-and-let-them-help-whom-they-please approach. Let us examine each of these approaches in more detail.

Direct Government Programs: Poverty

While women have been the targets of certain specific government programs, one particular set of programs has reached a large number of women—programs to aid people living below the poverty line. The overwhelming majority of poor people in America—two out of three—are women.[9] Why? To begin with, women's unemployment rates are much higher than men's, and women's earnings are much lower when they do find work. Poverty is less likely if a woman lives with a male wage-earner. If the couple breaks up, financial problems grow. But what about alimony? In 1978, only 25% of the women in this country received the amount that the court ordered, and the courts have not necessarily ordered generous amounts anyway.[10]

The female-headed household has been on the rise in recent years, especially in the poverty figures. As the government statisticians have summarized it:

> *In 1960 there were about 31 female-headed families for every 100 male-headed families below the poverty level, while in 1974 there were 85 female-headed families for every 100 male-headed families.*[11]

Since women's wages are so much lower than men's, it is not surprising that as the number of female-headed families rises, the proportion of female-headed families under the poverty line will also rise. In 1980, the average married-couple family earned $428 per week; the average female-headed family earned only $220 per week.[12]

The low pay of pink-collar work can be viewed as the starting point for explaining women's poverty-level incomes. Add to that women's unequal access to work-related benefits. Unemployment insurance benefits, for instance, are not paid to workers in household services, a major field of women's employment. Most unemployment benefits are paid only to workers willing but unable to find full-time work; since women form a disproportionate share of the part-time work force, there are exclusions from benefits in this fashion too.[13]

We have seen that more women than men experience poverty. Now let us turn to the government programs that deal with poverty problems. Since these programs tend to change a bit under each government administration, it would be tiresome to describe the particulars of specific programs that might not exist a few years later. Instead, we shall explore some of the basic principles underlying the programs, along with the critical variables in welfare policy.

Most welfare programs have two functions: to provide subsistence income for the unemployed and to provide them with some means of returning to paid employment so that welfare is no longer needed. For instance, the Aid to Families with Dependent Children (AFDC) program is aimed at female-headed families with below-poverty-level income, although the level of cash benefits is quite low. According to a 1975 study, "92 percent of the families receiving AFDC were poor before; 76 percent of AFDC families remain poor after receiving aid."[14]

To obtain AFDC money, recipients must register in the Work Incentive Program (WIN), which is supposed to help the AFDC mothers move from welfare to work. Specifically, it is supposed to train and place the welfare recipient in a job; in addition, child care is subsidized so that the AFDC mother can become self-supporting. Or can she? We must investigate these programs more closely. After the welfare recipient registers with WIN, or CETA, or any other agency, is she given job training? Is she trained for a job that pays living wages?

According to experts, "Those recipients who are able to find employment do not earn even a poverty-level wage."[15] Others have charged that our welfare programs actually discriminate against women, citing the higher spending levels of programs for male welfare recipients and the role of veterans's preference programs. Furthermore, they point out that public-service job training is usually rationed on a "one job to a family" basis, systematically favoring the unemployed father, when he is available.[16] This is frequently done by setting a family-income limitation on eligibility, so a woman whose husband is employed will be ineligible for public service employment. This is how the National Commission for Manpower Policy stated it:

> *It is inequitable to have individuals in families with secondary wage earners competing with unemployed family heads without regard to the total financial needs and resources of their respective families. An income ceiling for eligibility would be a spur to increasing the proportion of PSE (public service employment) jobs made available to disadvantaged persons.*[17]

While for most recipients the meager amount supplied by welfare payments is itself an adequate work incentive, the so-called workfare rules, which mandate registration for jobs, do very little to help women escape poverty. The training is usually minimal and the few job placements are usually for poverty-level jobs. When viewed within the context of the high unemployment rate in the United States, this is not surprising.

Of course, there are other government programs that provide economic assistance to women. Tax credits are available to middle- and upper-income women to defray a portion of their child-care expenses. Some states have displaced homemaker programs to help the widowed or divorced older woman adjust to a self-supporting life style. Women's apprenticeship programs have helped some women over the obstacles to entering some traditionally male occupations. In past years (although this has been eliminated recently), the federally financed Small Business Administration (SBA) has funded special assistance programs for women entrepreneurs. While many of these target programs have been effective, there is never any assurance that they will continue. Counterbalancing these useful direct-assistance programs, of course, are the government programs that penalize women as wives. These include our biased social security system, the unemployment compensation system, and the federal income tax system.[18] All of these tend to handicap the *second* wage earner of a family, which is usually the wife.

Government Macroeconomic Policy and the Unemployment Problem

AFDC, job training, and SBA loans are direct government programs that support women's economic needs. The major indirect approach to helping women is government macroeconomic policy. The theory here is quite simple. If the government pursues a policy of full employment, more men *and* women find it easier to gain employment. Also, all other thing being equal, fuller employment implies that more is produced, which can mean a higher standard of living for all workers. Since peacetime full employment policies have been quite rare, however, it is hard to evaluate their actual benefits. What we *have* seen is that when the government abandons the full employment objective in favor of other goals (as in the 1970s), unemployment increases. This has not only meant slower economic growth and lower economic welfare for all, but it has affected women and minority workers in a disproportionately severe fashion. In the period since World War II, women have entered the labor force in increasing numbers, but they have been disproportionately unemployed, as even the conservative data of Table 8-3 show.

Furthermore, as shown in Table 8-4, black and other minority women experience even higher unemployment rates. Recall that these are conservative estimates of unemployment, since they do not include the "discouraged workers," many of whom are women. The media may publicize the "liberated woman" and the special advantages of being "disadvantaged" these days, but the government's own statistics reveal the sad truth.

You may be wondering at this point why women experience this disproportionate unemployment burden. Why are women hit harder than men? While this is a difficult question to answer definitively, two explanations can be offered. On the one hand, when employers are hiring, they incorrectly decide that women "need" jobs less than men. Given the rising numbers of female-headed households and the estimate that half of all poor families are female-headed (refer to Note 11), this hiring bias is totally unjustified. Women *need* those jobs, just as men do.

A second explanation for the disproportionate impact of unemployment on women and minorities relates more directly to federal policy. Under the recent affirmative action approach mentioned ear-

TABLE 8-3
Unemployment Rates of Women and Men: Annual Averages
(Persons 16 Years of Age and Over)

Year	Number of Women Unemployed (in thousands)	Percentage of Labor Force Unemployed		
		Both Sexes	Women	Men
1979	2,945	5.8	6.8	5.1
1978	2,996	6.0	7.2	5.2
1977	3,267	7.0	8.2	6.2
1976	3,320	7.7	8.6	7.0
1975	3,445	8.5	9.3	7.9
1974	2,408	5.6	6.7	4.8
1973	2,064	4.9	6.0	4.1
1972	2,205	5.6	6.6	4.9
1971	2,217	5.9	6.9	5.3
1970	1,853	4.9	5.9	4.4
1969	1,428	3.5	4.7	2.8
1968	1,397	3.6	4.8	2.9
1967	1,468	3.8	5.2	3.1
1966	1,324	3.8	4.8	3.2
1965	1,452	4.5	5.5	4.0
1964	1,581	5.2	6.2	4.6
1963	1,598	5.7	6.5	5.2
1962	1,488	5.5	6.2	5.2
1961	1,717	6.7	7.2	6.4
1960	1,366	5.5	5.9	5.4
1959	1,320	5.5	5.9	5.3
1958	1,504	6.8	6.8	6.8
1957	1,018	4.3	4.7	4.1
1956	1,039	4.1	4.8	3.8
1955	998	4.4	4.9	4.2
1954	1,188	5.5	6.0	5.3*
1953	632	2.9	3.3	2.8
1952	698	3.0	3.6	2.8
1951	834	3.3	4.4	2.8
1950	1,049	5.3	5.7	5.1

Source: U.S. Department of Labor, Bureau of Labor Statistics, "Handbook of Labor Statistics, 1978," and "Employment and Earnings," January 1979 and 1980.

lier, many firms tried to locate and hire women and minorities. Yet this employment approach is extremely vulnerable to changes in the overall economic climate. A recession triggers "last hired, first fired" layoffs of women. As one economist has noted, recessions are not "equal opportunity dis-employers." If the government maintained a full employment economy, however, affirmative action hiring could become the basis for the greater integration of women in the labor

TABLE 8-4
Employment Status of Women by Race/Ethnic Group
(Numbers in Thousands)

	1979	1976
Women, 16 years and over:		
Civilian labor force	43,391	38,414
Employed	40,446	35,095
Unemployed	2,945	3,320
Unemployment rate (%)	6.8	8.6
Labor force participation rate (%)	51.0	47.3
White women, 16 years and over:		
Civilian labor force	37,528	33,371
Employed	35,304	30,739
Unemployed	2,224	2,632
Unemployment rate (%)	5.9	7.9
Labor force participation rate (%)	50.6	46.9
Black women, 16 years and over:		
Civilian labor force	4,984	4,369
Employed	4,324	3,748
Unemployed	660	621
Unemployment rate (%)	13.2	14.2
Labor force participation rate (%)	53.1	49.8
Other minority women, 16 years and over:		
Civilian labor force	879	675
Employed	817	608
Unemployed	62	67
Unemployment rate (%)	7.1	9.9
Labor force participation rate (%)	56.0	52.3

market on a long-term basis. Similarly, women's unemployment burden could be reduced and women's poverty status improved. In this sense, women and minorities have a greater stake in full employment economic policies than anyone else.

The New Theory of the Role of Government: Business Tax Cuts and Deregulation

Economists and public policy makers are increasingly turning away from this full employment government policy approach in favor of the third, indirect policy approach: let government aid business, and

TABLE 8-4
(continued)

	1979	1976
All Hispanic women, 20 years and over:		
Civilian labor force	1,731	1,408
Employed	1,577	1,246
Unemployed	154	162
Unemployment rate (%)	8.9	11.5
Labor force participation rate (%)	47.9	44.4
Mexican women, 20 years and over:		
Civilian labor force	989	753
Employed	892	664
Unemployed	98	89
Unemployment rate (%)	9.9	11.8
Labor force participation rate (%)	48.2	45.3
Puerto Rican women, 20 years and over:		
Civilian labor force	185	164
Employed	167	144
Unemployed	17	20
Unemployment rate (%)	9.3	12.1
Labor force participation rate (%)	35.3	32.0
Cuban women, 20 years and over:		
Civilian labor force	157	146
Employed	145	132
Unemployed	12	15
Unemployment rate (%)	7.9	9.9
Labor force participation rate (%)	55.1	50.7

Source: U.S. Department of Labor, Bureau of Labor Statistics, "Employment and Earnings," January 1976 and 1980.

business will aid whom it pleases. These so-called supply-side theorists demand government programs for industrial stimulus (business tax cuts and deregulation, for example), so that business will be more profitable than ever. Business profitability is then supposed to benefit all working people, on a kind of "trickle-down" basis.

While there are no guarantees that women or minorities will receive the "trickle," there are certain aspects of this approach that should affect all workers quite directly. First, deregulation will include less enforcement of looser occupational health and safety rules and environmental impact standards, which probably will mean more health problems for workers and residents in the vicinity of workplaces. Second, there will be less regulation of the right to unionize plants, so workers may find it more difficult to unionize without losing their jobs. Most important, however, the Equal Employment Opportunity Commission will have a sharply curtailed sphere of intervention, as employers are released from mandatory nondiscrimination regulations. All these aspects of the deregulation of business will probably make it more difficult for women and minority workers to work under safe conditions with nondiscriminatory pay and promotion rules.

The second part of the supply-side economic policy package has little to do with supply theory at all, yet it lies at the core of this whole program. The basic thrust of this redefinition of government policy is to increase sharply military expenditures and to decrease sharply government public services expenditures. When we consider the small proportion of women in the armed forces (about 6%) and the large proportion of women in other areas of government employment, this shift will have a disastrous impact on women's employment possibilities.

The Government as Employer

We have seen that the government, through its direct and indirect policies, and through its legislation, structures the economic environment of women. But we often forget that the government is a major employer too, much like private business. In fact, the government hires over 20% of all non-farm adult employed women, and the rate of growth of female employment in the federal civil service has increased rapidly since World War II. Does the government discriminate against women?

Look at the data in Table 8-5, which shows the percentage of women in different civil service levels from 1968 to 1976. The pattern of discrimination can be seen in the "grade groupings," since women are bunched in the low civil service grades and very few women have reached the higher-paid ranks. If we looked at the armed services, we would find much the same story; in fact, only recently have women been allowed entry to the upper echelons of the armed services. Looking at the government as an employer (and as a major employer of women workers), we see another layer of government policy toward women. Their own hiring procedures have confined women to the low-paid ranks of the civil service. And contrary to optimistic hopes for change, this government version of job segregation will be perpetuated in the future, with "job freeze" regulations and other budget-cutting plans.

TABLE 8-5
Full-Time White-Collar Employment[a] by GS and Equivalent Grade Grouping 1968–1970, 1972–1976
(Excluding U.S. Postal Service Pay Plans)

Grade Grouping		1968	1969	1970	1972	1973	1974[b]	1975[c]	1976
1–6	Total	596,244	570,937	556,223	582,193	577,559	588,430	584,605	561,765
	Women	438,841	417,376	403,729	411,291	410,653	419,039	418,756	408,727
	% Women	73.6	73.1	72.6	70.6	71.1	71.2	71.6	72.7
7–12	Total	584,568	606,957	609,957	623,565	615,300	618,815	641,044	644,639
	Women	125,593	134,253	138,489	146,917	148,773	158,427	171,840	181,114
	% Women	21.5	22.1	22.7	23.6	24.2	25.6	26.8	28.0
13 and above	Total	168,578	181,068	187,555	197,481	198,962	197,337	202,832	205,054
	Women	6,357	7,012	7,469	8,336	9,014	9,317	10,368	11,158
	% Women	3.8	3.9	4.0	4.2	4.5	4.7	5.1	5.4
Total	Total	1,349,390	1,358,805	1,353,735	1,403,239	1,391,821	1,404,582	1,428,481	1,411,458
	Women	570,791	558,641	549,687	566,544	568,440	586,783	600,964	600,999
	% Women	42.3	41.1	40.6	40.4	40.8	41.8	42.1	42.6

[a]Data are as of October 31 of each year, except in 1976, which is as of November 30. Data from 1971 are now shown due to differences in survey coverage.

[b]The 1974 data exclude 26,016 employees who are paid under white-collar pay plans that are not equivalent to the General Schedule.

[c]The 1975 data exclude 28,488 employees who are paid under white-collar pay plans that are not equivalent to the General Schedule.

Source: N. Benokraitis, "Employment Problems of Women: Federal Government Example," *in* K. Feinstein, ed., *Families and Working Women,* p. 227.

Conclusions

Our government's policies toward women do not present a picture of clear-cut goodwill or progress. As a lawmaker, as an economic policy maker, and as a major employer, the U.S. government does not seem to have done too much to help its women citizens. Target programs to aid specific groups of the population, such as the poor, have not seemed to help poor women significantly. Other programs, such as unemployment insurance or social security, have been found to discriminate against certain classes of women. And macroeconomic policy has not done much to bolster women's chances of finding jobs. On the contrary, women's unemployment and poverty have soared. Antidiscrimination laws, which could be quite powerful, have been rendered impotent by a lack of enforcement. Ultimately, the government has proved unwilling to challenge business's (profitable) discriminatory behavior. Finally, as if things were not bad enough already, the government's *own* discrimination record as an employer undermines the credibility of its "commitment" to women's needs.

Additional Readings

For a good background on the legal protections against discrimination, see M. Eastwood's "Legal Protection Against Sex Discrimination," in A. Stromberg and S. Harkess, *Women Working*. A lengthier review of the legal system is given in E. Cary and K. Peratis, *Women and the Law*. On welfare, read D. Pearce, "Women, Work and Welfare: The Feminization of Poverty," *in* K. Feinstein, ed., *Working Women and Families*. For an in-depth look at sex discrimination in public service employment, see L. Underwood, *Women in Federal Employment Programs* (Urban Institute, 1979).

Notes

1. This was a case before the War Labor Board and GE and Westinghouse in 1945. See W. Newman's "Presentation" *in* M. Blaxall and B. Reagan, *Women and the Workplace*, p. 267.
2. *Ibid.*
3. *Ibid*, p. 271.
4. This is in the case of *Weeks v. Southern Bell Telephone and Telegraph Co.*, quoted by M. Eastwood, "Legal Protection Against Sex Discrimination," *in* A. Stromberg and S. Harkess, *Women Working*, p. 116.
5. "A Breakthrough Case on Women's Pay Bias," *Business Week*, September 8, 1980, p. 42.

6. Quoted by M. Eastwood, p. 117.

7. *Employment Goals of the World Plan of Action: Developments and Issues in the United States* (Women's Bureau, 1980), p. 24.

8. "A Business Group Fights 'Comparable Worth,' " *Business Week,* November 10, 1980, p. 100.

9. D. Pearce, "Women, Work and Welfare: The Feminization of Poverty," *in* K. Feinstein, ed., *Working Women and Families,* p. 103.

10. *White House News on Women,* Vol. II, #8, December 1980.

11. U.S. Bureau of the Census, *A Statistical Portrait of Women in the U.S.* (1976), p. 46.

12. BLS Report #611, "Employment in Perspective: Working Women," July 1980, p. 1.

13. Pearce, *op cit,* p. 111.

14. Quoted in Pearce, *op cit,* p. 113.

15. Pearce, p. 119.

16. L. Underwood, *Women in Federal Employment Programs,* Urban Institute, 1979.

17. Quoted in *ibid,* p. 21.

18. See *Employment Goals of the World Plan of Action: Developments and Issues in the United States* (Women's Bureau, 1980), pp. 31–33, for a brief summary.

The Business World and Working Women

How does the business world view the working woman of today? Do businessmen still look at women workers as cheap, docile, skilled labor as they did in the nineteenth century? Have discrimination lawsuits by crusading activists and back-pay awards to masses of litigating working women changed businessmen's minds about women workers? If women workers can no longer be underpaid, will they still be hired? Or are women now successful members of the executive elite? These are some of the bottom-line questions that are being asked today, in spite of the mass media assumption that women workers have already "made it." How *does* the business world view the new woman?

What Is Meant by "The Business World"?

There is a difference between individual businessmen, with their particular attitudes and practices, and the business community as a group, with positions and policies articulating the interests of businessmen at large. The business world includes feminist businesses and mom-and-pop businesses, as well as large multinational corporations. Certain businesses may have a very paternalistic approach to their women workers, providing good fringe benefits or pregnancy

143

disability leaves, for example. Others may treat their women workers as an undifferentiated mass of low-wage workers and express very little interest in sex-related work issues.

As varied as the particular firms may seem, there is a common level or community of interests that operates in the business world, representing the interests of business at large. There are organizations—the National Association of Manufacturers, the various chambers of commerce, and the Equal Employment Advisory Council, to name a few—which have been created and supported by businessmen to address the concerns of business. Some provide forums for individual businesses to express their needs and interests, others research issues of interest to members, and still others lobby local and national politicians to support their causes. These organizations exist to express the interests of business as a group, so it is *their* positions on the working woman that must be examined in some detail.

The Business Community and the Pregnancy Question

Take the issue of pregnancy leave for women workers. Many individual firms have provided quite equitable policies toward their women workers on pregnancy-related benefits. IBM, for instance, treats pregnancy as a normal disability and grants the worker up to a year of fully paid disability leave after childbirth. Several firms have this policy. Yet when the U.S. House of Representatives Subcommittee on Employment Opportunities held hearings on amendments to Title VII of the Civil Rights Act to prohibit sex discrimination on the basis of pregnancy, the business community testified against the amendments. The Chamber of Commerce representative, for instance, started by introducing the Chamber of Commerce as "the largest association of business and professional organizations in the United States" and the "principal spokesman for the American business community. . . ," representing "over 3,500 trade associations and chambers of commerce" with "a direct membership of over 62,000 business firms."[1] He then went on to explain why business was opposed to treating pregnancy as any other physical disability. His main point was that this law would increase costs for firms having "a large proportion of female employees," firms that also "tend to pay lower wages,"[2] implying that pink-collar industries could not survive the cost of this proposed amendment, since their profitability was based on employing masses of cheap, female workers. While he also tried to raise the specter of legal complications that could arise from covering pregnancy as a work disability (including the fantasy of children suing employers for fetal injuries their mothers might have suffered while employed),[3] his basic argument was financial—business did not want to pay the extra money.

While some business organizations confined themselves to a blunt rejection of the financial burden, others expressed themselves more broadly on how they see working women today. The National Retail Merchants Association (representing 33,000 retailers) first stated its opposition: "Adoption of such legislation would have a particularly severe adverse financial impact upon the retail industry where between 80 and 85 percent of all employees are women."[4] They went on to state their view of why women work: ". . . These women are not the primary breadwinners in their families, but are people who take jobs in retailing to supplement the family's primary source of income or to earn extra spending money."[5] Then they brought out their theory of pregnancy: "Pregnancy is normally a voluntary, planned-for event, financially easier to cope with than illness or accident . . . when a woman becomes pregnant, she and her family are usually able to prepare for the expected jolt to her earning power."[6] Another view of the working woman came from the National Association of Manufacturers (representing over 13,000 employers): "The truth is that women who bear children have not consistently indicated such an interest in a continuing career."[7]

The business community routinely speaks as a group, presenting their theories about working women and about a wide range of issues related to women. They also inform our lawmakers as to their financial interests in these issues. Their message is quite clear: they are opposed to legislation that will impose any increased costs on their operations. Most antidiscrimination or equal benefits legislation will cost business some money. Business groups oppose such legislation even if they have to resort to outdated theories of why women work, such as the old "pin money" story resurrected by the National Retail Merchants Association.

Pregnancy disability coverage is not even the most critical working women's issue being debated today. Occupational health policies, because they involve potentially expensive lawsuits, are a particularly volatile set of issues, as are unionization rights. But the hottest area is probably the "equal pay for comparable worth" battle.

The Business Community and the Comparable Worth Problem

Women's movement advocates have long been aware that the 1963 Equal Pay Act did not go far enough to eliminate wage discrimination in America, since it addressed only the narrowest definition of discrimination: men and women doing the same (or "substantially similar") work but receiving unequal pay. The most typical form of discrimination in our sex-segregated economy is that certain jobs pay less not because the work is less skilled or less demanding, but because the jobs are filled by women. In these jobs, there may not be any basis for an equal pay claim for women, simply because there may not be any men in these low-paying positions. The "equal pay for work of comparable worth" concept is the first antidiscrimination campaign that recognizes the role of occupational sex segregation in compounding the effects of wage discrimination.

The business community has decided to attack the comparable worth campaign with its full forces. In 1976 they created the Equal Employment Advisory Council (EEAC) "to deal specifically with government affirmative action policies," with a budget of $1 million "funded mainly by annual dues of $5,000 from each member."[8] While its membership is secret, the board of directors includes representatives of "GE, Exxon, Sears, General Motors," and others.[9] This group not only researches the business stance on affirmative action proposals, but advises lobbyists and publishes position papers. It credits itself with a few of the major business victories that limit antibias cases, particularly in the area of seniority preference rules and in the limitation of "class action" suits, but their biggest target is the comparable worth struggle. Realizing that "billions in payroll dollars"[10] are at stake, they are trying to argue that the "market" will aid working women more than legislation will, legislation which they characterize as ill defined and unrelated to bias anyway. This battle may indeed be the decisive test of whether working women will be provided with a legal basis for equal pay demands.

How Business Adjusts to Antidiscrimination Laws

While the business community lobbies for the types of employee policies that it, as a group, wants passed, within individual firms different considerations may dictate a variety of policies. Two broad objectives govern most firms' employee policies, irrespective of the sex of the workers in question. Most firms want to retain, as much as possible, their managerial prerogatives: the right to hire, to fire, or to reassign their workers as they see fit. And, of course, they want to gain the maximum output from each worker at the minimum cost.

The business community's first objective—to retain managerial prerogatives—has been somewhat threatened by federal antidiscrimination legislation in recent years. Management can no longer ask sex-biased questions on job application forms (although most firms still do). Until recent changes made by the Reagan administration, if a firm was a federal contractor, it had to set targets for affirmative action hiring, although the firm was bound only to "good faith efforts" to meet those targets with actual hires. Other legislation has stipulated that once a woman employee is hired, a firm cannot discriminate against her in terms of pay, promotion, or firing decisions. If most firms had to take these regulations seriously, they would experience a great erosion of their traditional rights to "manage." As we saw in Chapter 8, however, most firms do not find these federal regulations too intimidating. Not only are the penalties and the probability of conviction low, but many firms find ways to *appear* as if they are complying with the law without actually doing so.

How can firms appear to comply with affirmative action guidelines without disturbing their overall managerial autonomy? Clearly, this issue is most sensitive at the managerial level, since women in these posts can affect important policy decisions. Ever since affirmative action was mandated, firms have found it easiest to fill the requirement for women at top echelons by hiring women for their public relations departments, the "velvet ghetto" of business.[11] Hiring women in the PR departments pushes up the number of affirmative action hires for the Equal Employment Opportunity Commission (EEOC) compliance reports, even though these women find their so-called management-level positions dead ended. Unlike other high echelon posts, there is no route from the PR department into general corporate management. In fact, a recent survey indicates that women make up less than 5% of the managers earning $40,000 per year or more in America's top 50 industrial firms.[12] Corporations have found the "numbers game" a convenient way to keep women out of top management, where their presence is potentially problematic if they are vested with the usual managerial decision-making powers.

The case of the managerial woman will be explored in more depth later in this chapter. What about the average white-collar or blue-collar woman worker? Before the equal pay and civil rights acts, firms *did* hire many women. Realizing their high productivity, businesses hired women and paid them less than men, earning the company higher profits. After equal pay laws were passed, firms were faced with three choices. They could sacrifice some profits and pay women equal wages for equal work. Or they could reclassify men's and women's jobs so they no longer appeared equal. Or, as the third alternative, they could simply keep discriminating and pay any fines they might ultimately be charged. For most firms, this has simply been another cost minimization question. They have chosen the least expensive alternative.

Relative Aptitudes of Male and Female Workers

Apart from legal considerations, however, firms do realize that their women employees are quite productive: they are well educated, skilled, and potentially very loyal to the firm. For the last 50 years, industrial studies of the relative aptitudes of male and female workers have provided scientific evidence for the productivity of women workers. Researchers have found, for instance, that there are no discernible differences in the aptitudes of the sexes in 14 key skills, ranging from analytical and inductive reasoning to pitch discrimination and tweezer dexterity. On the other hand, women are found to surpass men in six skill areas (finger dexterity, accounting aptitudes, "ideaphoria," observation, silograms, and abstract visualization), while men surpass women in two areas (grip and structural visualization).[13]

Although women's skill aptitudes would seem to mean that women can be as productive as men, some on-site researchers urge caution. Industrial ergonomists who have tested workers' physical work efficiency on the shop floor itself have found women less productive than men because the equipment has been designed to accommodate a male physique.[14] In other words, women's high marks for skill aptitude in the laboratory tests do not always carry through on the production floor, since women may be using tools that were designed for male workers.

Relative Costs of Male and Female Workers

Even though women workers can be as productive as male workers, they usually cost the employer less, in terms of both benefits and pure wages. Studies of employee disability costs have shown that, on the average, male workers receive higher disability benefits and stay out of work longer than women workers.[15] Employers have also found that married women workers, already covered by their husbands' benefits packages, do not need relatively expensive fringe benefits, such as life or health insurance. Corporate officials, who call this "coordination of benefits," have already saved themselves some money this way.[16] Not only are the fringe benefits for the married woman employee less costly to a firm, but many industries look for married women workers in order to pay lower wages. As a corporate director of a major electronic parts company stated:

> *In the 38-year history of the company I work for, it has historically employed secondary wage earners. We are not a high paying industry. Now, that historically has been women.... When we employ people and on their application they indicate that their spouse works somewhere else, or they are re-entering the work force, or they are entering it for the first time, I consider them a secondary wage earner in the home.*[17]

While businesses look for secondary wage earners because they do not intend to pay high wages, they are also adamantly opposed to the provision of pregnancy disability leave, which can be seen as the "flip side" of hiring secondary wage earners. On the one hand firms want married women with employed husbands, since their wage requirements are usually lower, but on the other hand they do not want to cover their workers' pregnancy disabilities.

This is only a single instance of a much broader problem the business community faces in its dual involvement with women. Their women workers are valuable, highly productive employees. A large sector of American industry relies on the low-wage labor of women. Yet on the other hand the women of this country are supposed to manage the consumption of the goods that business produces, as well as to bear and raise the future labor force. When women challenge this double burden, refusing to work at their jobs all day and then do the housework at night, business can have some problems.

The Woman as Worker *and* Consumer: New Contradictions

Traditionally, business has dealt with women's double burden by studiously ignoring it. In business advertising, women have been portrayed as full-time housewives; they are in their homes selling a product found in the kitchen or bathroom. Recently, however, many firms have tried to recapture the working women market with their "double burden streamliners," expensive computerized household equipment that "thinks." Working women, according to the ads, can buy their right to a career by purchasing microwave ovens, food processors, or programmable washing machines—appliances that will do everything the working woman does not have time to do anymore. Playing on the traditional feeling of guilt over the undone chores, industry has tried to sell women on a "high-tech" solution to the housework problem.

The main problem with this high-tech alternative is that it is also quite expensive, and most women take paid labor-market jobs because they do not have enough money in the first place. This may account for the present-day revolution in marketing that has shocked the industry experts: the growth of no-frills grocery stores and generic (unbranded) merchandise. Working women seem to have found their own answer to part of the double burden by buying these cheaper generic goods. With generic products, women's low wages can stretch as much as 30% further. In addition, the growth of generic buying indicates that shoppers are rejecting a lot of the mystification of housework. Doubly burdened working women, in their brandless shopping, seem to be rejecting the entire concept of housework as a way for women to prove themselves as "real women." As one marketing industry expert recently commented:

> *It used to be status among women to know the best brands in the supermarket, but that's not an arena for Brownie points anymore....* [18]

Indeed, the business world may be forced to take a second look at the overworked and underpaid working women. These women may be starting some quiet revolutions on their own.

What about the better-paid executive women? Is life sweeter at the top? We will turn now to the very different case of the corporate woman.

The Corporate Woman: Silver Lining of Our Cloud?

There is a great deal of talk these days about the "corporate woman." Women's magazines have regular columns of advice on the psychological intricacies of management careers.[19] The *New York Times* has featured full-color spreads on the woman executive's office decor.[20]

The *Times* interviewers have talked with top female executives on the pressing problems of make-up that will stay fresh during those long board meetings and of hairdressers that will do "touchups" at inconvenient hours.[21] A mini-industry of upward-mobility counseling for women has mushroomed in recent years. Indeed, America has created its latest success model, the corporate woman. An updated, female version of the Horatio Alger hero, she is smart, hard working, and lucky. She is shown as living proof to all of us that the free enterprise system really works, that women can move upward if they try hard enough. According to this new version of the old myth, the best women *can* work their way to the top. Furthermore, the women's magazines suggest, as these women move to the top they will help other qualified women to rise as well. To mix metaphors a bit, as the cream of working women rise to the top, they will leaven the whole loaf. All women will benefit, then, from the hard-won success of their talented sisters. It is an appealing story for many women, but is there any truth in it? Let us examine some of the evidence.

Unequal Pay and Promotion for Corporate Women

There are actually two types of corporate women, those who have corporate positions in major industrial enterprises and those who own their own businesses. Since they are very different types of women, we shall begin with the women employed by major corporations in executive positions. These women *do* earn much more than other working women and their jobs have higher status, with better fringe benefits and greater promotion possibilities. Yet, by the standards of the corporate world, these women are "second class citizens."

All major surveys of executive pay have shown that women managers earn a lot less than their male counterparts.[22] As the *Wall Street Journal* reported from a 1980 survey, 30% of women executives earn less than $30,000 per year and 60% earn less than $50,000; male executives average $134,500 per annum.[23] According to another survey, women make up less than 5% of the executives earning more than $40,000 per year in the country's top 50 industrial firms.[24]

Some optimists might try to explain women's low earnings on the basis of their relatively recent entry into the managerial ranks. Yet researchers studying recent entrants have found this low-wage pattern persisting. A study of Columbia University M.B.A. graduates found that males and females started their management careers with roughly similar salaries ($12,414 for the women and $13,692 for the men in 1969), but that ten years later the gap for this same cohort of graduates had widened considerably ($34,036 for the women and $48,900 for the men in 1979).[25] A study of Harvard M.B.A. graduates has revealed similar findings.[26]

In the business world, pay increases are fairly accurate proxies for corporate upward mobility. The lower salaries of corporate women reflect their limited promotion prospects. As one study concluded, "forty percent of the male managers argued that a woman has virtually no chance of getting to the top of the managerial elite."[27]

Harassment and Insecurity

In addition to getting paid less and facing more limited promotion possibilities than their male peers, corporate women find life on the job quite grim. A recent *Harvard Business Review* survey indicates that sexual harassment is a major problem for women, particularly for those who want to advance in their firms. Women trying to work their way up in the corporate world still find that the price may be "sexual favors." As one male executive candidly admitted, "there is a male code of silence regarding harassment of females that has to be broken, particularly in the area of male 'power' figures and females without power."[28] One woman manager remarked, ". . . women are 'expected' to have to cope with that type of behavior."[29] Indeed, 59% of the male executives surveyed thought that "a smart woman employee ought to have no trouble handling an unwanted sexual approach."[30] Overall, the survey indicates that the problem of sexual harassment is still pervasive, even if there are more women in the corporate world than ever before.

Furthermore, corporate women may find that occupational success itself may be quite precarious. In 1980, two of the most successful corporate women, Jane Pfeiffer of NBC and Mary Cunningham of Bendix, lost their jobs in a blaze of publicity. Cunningham resigned after "malicious gossip" about her relationship with her mentor, the president of Bendix, made it impossible for her to work effectively. This was clearly a case of the double standard: young men who rise quickly are admired for their ambition, but young women are accused of sexual dirty tricks if they rise too quickly. The moral was obvious: "Executive women, like Caesar's wife, must in fact be above reproach."[31] Setting aside all the mythology of women's advancement, it is clear that some things have not changed. If a woman is successful, she will be accused of sexual misconduct, even if she has her Harvard M.B.A.

Why Corporate Women Have Such a Hard Time

It is easier to debunk the myth of women's corporate success than it is to explain why women have not "made it." A 1972 survey of managerial attitudes toward women as executives may give some clues.[32] A majority of respondents, for instance, thought that women had higher turnover rates than men. This attitude is unusual, since few firms even *keep* turnover statistics by sex and most continually complain that their bright young men are bid away from them.

Apart from the turnover complaint, managers seem to think women are less "committed" to careers and less competitive than men. In addition, they are viewed as having higher absenteeism rates and as being resented by other workers, especially if they are in supervisory positions. On the other hand, most managers did *not* feel women were less decisive, less aggressive, less independent, or less productive than men.[33] It all adds up to a fairly inconclusive and inconsistent assessment of the woman manager.

Recently, some experts have offered more interesting insights into the career advancement difficulties of corporate women. Much of the problem seems to be due to the attitudes of male bosses themselves:

> ... *increasingly, companies and consultants believe tensions between male bosses and female subordinates are a major reason for the disparity. Corporate advancement is heavily dependent on a boss's approval, and for reasons not their fault, women mightn't get the support they need from male superiors.*[34]

This sentiment is echoed throughout the literature. Women may have new careers, but many men "refuse to cope with today's corporate reality—women in the board room."[35] Women face male resistance from their superiors as well as from their subordinates, and they even receive it from their husbands. Some executive women have given up hope of finding a husband who can accept a wife with competitive career ambitions, which they see as crucial for their success. As a recent study of "corporate husbands" acknowledged:

> *One solution for women is to opt out of marriage. Indeed, top echelon women are predominantly never married, or married with no children. ... The message to executive women ... is clear: Find a man of quality who is not threatened by women of equality.*[36]

On the mundane side, the *Wall Street Journal* notes:

Nearly two-thirds of married women officers at 1,300 big concerns spend more than 10 hours weekly on home chores, says a study by Heidrick & Struggles, executive recruiters. But about an equal proportion of their husbands spend less than 10 hours weekly on such tasks.[37]

Compounding women's problems with the men at work and the men at home are those particular remnants of past discrimination that "cramp the style" of executive women. The Equal Credit Opportunity Act was passed five years ago, but women still face discrimination at their bank's loan offices and from credit card companies.[38] Women are still barred from membership or even guest privileges at many private clubs, where executive level business is often transacted.[39] How can a woman be an effective corporate executive when she cannot join the men for lunch?

A Different Managerial Style

While women face many sex-related obstacles to success in their corporate careers, there are some indications that women do not advance as easily as men because they have a characteristically different management style. Men favor an "exploitative style," working their subordinates hard and taking all the credit for that work themselves so they look good to their superiors. Women, it is felt, rarely use this obviously successful approach. Instead, they may favor the "task-oriented" approach, focusing on the work goals with little interest in the employees. Or, some women may use the "detached" approach, delegating all the work in an orderly fashion, but remaining personally aloof.

Most often, however, women seem to favor the "receptive" style, where the job gets done, but the manager *herself* has become involved with the workers and the work itself. These bosses are well liked by their subordinates, but "men in management expressed dismay at this particular 'female' style of running an office."[40] Although this "female" management style is quite effective, generating employee loyalty while ensuring task efficiency, it wins no applause from upper management. Other studies have found that women managers seem much less "money oriented," which may also fit in with the more cooperative management style that women favor.[41]

If these various observations are indeed accurate, it may indicate there are more structural reasons why women do not succeed in the corporate game. They may be bringing different values to the workplace.

Self-Employed Business Women

A study of women's business potential would be incomplete without a look at the self-employed business woman. The woman business entrepreneur in America is quite different from the employed corporate woman, even if they are sometimes lumped together by the "success" magazines. Unlike the young woman climbing the corporate ladder, the woman entrepreneur is typically in her mid-forties, and she earns less than both salaried women and self-employed men.[42] Normally, she has been in the work force many years before starting her business (43% have been working at least 21 years), but not as a manager (only 13.4% were managers for 21 years and less than half have had any managerial jobs).[43] Most of these women started their own businesses, rather than inheriting them, and did it for the typical entrepreneurial reasons: to make money, to use their skills, and to be self-employed.[44]

While their businesses are small, and clustered in the low-profit retail or service sectors, they are remarkably successful. Over a third of the women entrepreneurs in the American Management Association survey reported that their business became profitable within the first year of operation.[45] Yet they do not limit their notion of success to the narrow criterion of profits. Since a majority of self-employed business women are married, "success" for them is a combination of a profitable business, a good marriage, and community work as well.

Their ability to combine family and career may be due, in part, to their relative maturity. As well as having worked for a long time before setting out in their own businesses, most of these women had stable family situations by that time. Perhaps they also benefit from being self-employed, since they do not have to cope with unnecessary opposition from male superiors. Since few have paid employees, they probably face little resistance from subordinates as well. Women entrepreneurs seem to face the most resistance, if they face any at all, from the banking community and from their business suppliers.[46] Apart from difficulties in arranging financing, these women seem to be fairly satisfied with their ability to operate autonomously, especially when compared to the women struggling their way up corporate ladders.

Conclusions

Given the degree of flux and uncertainty in the corporate world itself, it is hard to render a final verdict on the "new corporate woman." She faces wage and promotion discrimination as well as a lot of male opposition. She could neutralize her female handicap by adopting a more "male" style and by learning to cope with standard male opposition. Many of the studies of the new corporate woman advise just such a strategy. Two leading experts, for instance, stress that the aspiring woman's most critical step is:

> ... *the decision whether one really wants to succeed in a management career, a career that requires competing primarily with men, and competing with them in a system they understand better and on terms with which they are far more comfortable and much more familiar.*[47]

If so, they advise, "one can learn to manage one's personality."[48]

Alternatively, women can reject this total conformity to the male corporate world, since the corporate world itself "has already exhausted its potential for providing even acceptable work for most male managerial talent. . . ."[49] Women could instead promote their own managerial style, the cooperative method mentioned earlier. Or, women with entrepreneurial ambitions might well follow the self-employed route, which seems to offer more flexibility and autonomy, even if the financial rewards are lower. At least the choices today seem to be clearer, even if the roads are filled with obstacles.

Additional Readings

While there is a plethora of "success" books for women, describing the corporate ascent strategy, there are very few objective book-length studies of the business world's attitude toward the working woman. One study, which is somewhat old, but still interesting, is *Exploitation from 9 to 5: Report of the Twentieth Century Fund Task Force on Women and Employment* (Lexington Books, 1975). Readers should keep an eye on the *Wall Street Journal* and *Business Week* for their frequent articles on women. In fact, old *Business Week* articles, such as "The Corporate Woman: Up the Ladder, Finally" (*Business Week,* November 24, 1975), can still make very interesting reading.

Readers may appreciate the range of opinions expressed in the collection of readings in E. Ginzberg and A. Yohalem, *Corporate Lib: Women's Challenge to Management* (Johns Hopkins Press, 1973). A more technical analysis is offered in J. Lyle and J. Ross, *Women in Industry: Employment Patterns of Women in Corporate America* (Lexington Books, 1973). For a look at the adjust-and-succeed school of thought, see M. Hennig and A. Jardim, *The Managerial Woman* (Anchor, 1977). For more information on the self-employed business woman, see *The Bottom Line: Unequal Enterprise in America,* Report of the President's Interagency Task Force on Women Business Owners, 1978.

Notes

1. Hearing before the Subcommittee on Employment Opportunities of the Committee on Education and Labor of the House of Representatives, 95th Congress; Washington, D.C., April 6, 1977, Part I, p. 84.

2. *Ibid*, p. 86.

3. *Ibid*, p. 84.

4. *Ibid*, p. 252.

5. *Ibid*, p. 255.

6. *Ibid*.

7. *Ibid*, Part II, p. 82.

8. "A Business Group Fights 'Comparable Worth,'" *Business Week,* November 10, 1980, p. 100.

9. *Ibid*, p. 105.

10. *Ibid*, p. 100.

11. See "PR: 'The Velvet Ghetto' of Affirmative Action," *Business Week,* May 8, 1978, p. 122.

12. See "Few Women Get Top Business Jobs Despite Progress of Past Decade," *Wall Street Journal* 7/25/80.

13. J. Durkin, "The Potential of Women," reprinted in B. Stead, *Women in Management,* pp. 42–46. Ideaphoria measures the "rate of flow of ideas used in activities involving persuasion and verbal fluency. . ."; a silogram "measures the ability to easily form associations between known and unknown words. . . ."

14. "Manager's Journal," *Wall Street Journal* 7/28/80.

15. For data that *includes* pregnancy disability payments and still shows male employees more expensive than female employees, see evidence from Hawaii, *Hearings,* Part I, p. 214.

16. "New Benefits for New Lifestyles," *Business Week,* February 11, 1980.

17. This is testimony of the corporate director of AVX Ceramics of AVX Corporation, *Hearings,* Part II, p. 57.

18. "No-Frills Food: New Power for the Supermarkets," *Business Week,* March 23, 1981, p. 76.

19. See *Working Women* or other such magazines.

20. "Women's Ways with Executive Suites," *New York Times Magazine,* August 10, 1980.

21. "Keeping a Fresh Face at the Office," *New York Times Magazine,* August 10, 1980.

22. For example, see the results of a 1972 survey in J. Lyle and J. Ross, *Women in Industry,* p. 80.

23. "Women Managers Get Paid Far Less Than Males, Despite Career Gains," *Wall Street Journal* 10/7/80.

24. "Few Women Get Top Business Jobs Despite Progress of Past Decade," *Wall Street Journal* 7/25/80.

25. *Ibid.*

26. W. Robertson, "Women M.B.A.'s, Harvard—How They're Doing," *Fortune,* August 28, 1978, p. 54.

27. J. Lyle and J. Ross, p. 85.

28. Collins and Blodgett, "Sexual Harassment, Some See It . . . Some Won't," *Harvard Business Review,* March/April 1981, pp. 80, 81.

29. *Ibid,* p. 82.

30. *Ibid,* p. 90.

31. J. Adams, "Fallen Idols," *Working Woman,* January 1981, p. 64.

32. Lyle and Ross, p. 87.

33. *Ibid.*

34. "Women Trained to Gain Trust of Male Bosses," *Wall Street Journal* 1/16/81.

35. Adams, p. 99.

36. "Corporate Husbands" (Manager's Journal), *Wall Street Journal* 9/28/80.

37. "Who Washes Dishes," *Wall Street Journal* 9/23/80.

38. "Women Still Have a Hard Time Getting Credit," *Business Week,* December 1, 1980.

39. "Philadelphia Battle Over All-Male Clubs Reflects a Wider Dispute," *New York Times* 2/1/81.

40. Lyle and Ross, p. 90.

41. Robertson, p. 60.

42. *The Bottom Line: Unequal Enterprise in America,* Report of the President's Interagency Task Force on Women Business Owners, 1978, p. 31.

43. *Ibid,* p. 34.

44. *Ibid.*

45. The American Management Association's survey report is appended to *The Bottom Line.* For the information on business success, see p. 215.

46. *Ibid,* p. 213.

47. M. Hennig and A. Jardim, *The Managerial Woman,* p. 158.

48. *Ibid,* p. 159.

49. C. de Carlo, "The Larger Stakes," *in* E. Ginzberg and A. Yohalem, *Corporate Lib: Women's Challenge to Management,* p. 135.

The Trade Unions and Working Women

In most modern industrial countries, it would be unthinkable to discuss the conditions of any class of workers without referring to the activities of the trade union movement. Trade unions, after all, are supposed to represent workers' interests in an organized fashion, bargaining with employers over wages, hours of work, and working conditions. Yet in the United States, where only 20% of the total work force is unionized and only 11% of the female labor force is unionized, can the same claims be made? In what sense is trade unionism important for women workers in this country? While these are complex questions, the initial responses can be fairly straightforward.

The Impact of Unionization on Wages

Unionized workers have contracts that stipulate their working conditions, their job rights, their grievance procedures, and their wages. Nonunionized workers may not be covered by any such agreements, their working conditions may be extremely precarious, and their wages are usually much lower. Look at the data in Table 10-1, which shows the median earnings ratios of male and female workers in the different sectors of the work force according to their union status.

In 1970, male union workers averaged 30% higher wages than nonunion men, overall. In the blue-collar trades, union men earned

TABLE 10-1
Ratio of Median Earnings: 1970

| | Men to Women | | Union Members to Nonunion Workers | |
	Union	Nonunion	Men	Women
White-collar workers	1.8	2.8	0.9	1.4
Blue-collar workers	2.0	1.9	1.6	1.5
Operatives	1.9	1.8	1.6	1.5
Service workers	1.7	2.2	2.6	3.3
Total	2.0	2.5	1.3	1.7

Source: E. Raphael, "Working Women and Their Membership in Labor Unions," *Monthly Labor Review,* May 1974, p. 28.

60% more than nonunion men, and among service workers, union men made 160% more. While unionized workers usually receive higher wages, for women the differential is even more important. True, unions do not eliminate the sexual wage gap; overall, union men earn 100% more than union women. Yet among the nonunionized workers, males earn 150% more than females. Thus the gap is narrower among unionized workers. Looking just at the women workers, it is clear that union women earn more than nonunion women (70% more), and in some sectors, such as service work, union women earn much more than nonunion women (230% more).

While these statistics are certainly compelling, they do not explain *why* any of these differentials exist. Do the better-paid workers unionize, or do unions obtain better pay for what would have been low-paid workers? Why do union men earn more than union women, even if their wage gap is smaller than in the nonunion sector? While the earnings differences seem important, they cannot be understood independently of the membership data.

Women's Membership in the Union Movement

As mentioned before, a relatively small proportion of the U.S. labor force is unionized: roughly 20% of the total labor force and 25% of the nonagricultural labor force. This small proportion has been declining in recent years, in large part due to the rise of white-collar work in America, which unions have been less successful at entering. Since women workers are concentrated in those white-collar sectors, women's overall unionization rate has remained low (11%). Yet women form a rising proportion of the total membership of the union movement in America. While women made up only 18.3% of union membership in 1960, by 1978 they represented 24.2% of all union members. Furthermore, if all employee associations, such as the National Education Association (NEA) and the American Nurses Association (ANA), are included with the unions, women formed 28.1% of total membership by 1978.[1]

Although women are becoming an important growth factor for the unions and associations, they hold very few of the leadership positions in their unions. Table 10-2 lists the major unions with large female memberships, along with the percentage of females in the total membership and the percentage of females who are officers or governing board members of their unions.

While the employee associations have predominantly female membership and female leaderships, the unions have less representative leaderships. The Communication Workers union, with over 50% female membership, has no women on its board; the International Ladies' Garment Workers union has an 80% female membership, but a mere 7% female leadership. Just recently was a woman finally elected to the AFL–CIO Executive Council—the highest level policy-making body of the labor organization in America—and only after much debate and rule twisting. It has been estimated that women hold only 5% of all union offices in America, even though they make up 24% of the union membership.[2]

The exclusion of women from the leadership positions of the union movement may account for women's lower unionization rates; the employee associations, with their high levels of female leadership, seem to have increased their total female membership dramatically (80% increase in female membership from 1970 to 1976).[3] Beyond the sheer numbers, the lack of female leadership in the American trade union movement may indicate a more severe problem: the insensitivity of the organized labor movement to the needs of their women workers. For a perspective on this problem, a brief review of the history of organized labor's attitudes to women workers will be useful.

The Historical Roots of Women's Isolation from Unions

As indicated in Chapter 3, the background of bitterness between women and the unions in America can be traced to the philosophy of labor organizing that developed during our early industrialization

TABLE 10-2
Women's Union Leadership

	Total Membership	Women as a Percentage of the Total Membership	Percentage of Women Officers or Governing Board Members
Amalgamated Clothing and Textile Workers Union	501,000	66	15
American Federation of Government Employees	266,000	49	0
American Federation of State, County, and Municipal Employees	1,020,000	40	3
American Federation of Teachers	500,000	60	25
Communication Workers of America	508,063	51	0
Hotel, Restaurant Employees and Bartenders Union	430,000	42	4
International Association of Machinists and Aerospace Workers	920,735	13	0
International Brotherhood of Electrical Workers	1,011,725	30	0
International Brotherhood of Teamsters	1,923,896	25	0
International Ladies' Garment Workers	348,380	80	7
International Union of Electrical, Radio and Machine Workers (IUE)	255,427	40	4
Service Employees International Union	625,000	50	15
United Auto Workers	1,499,425	11	3
United Food and Commercial Workers	1,235,500	39	3
United Steel Workers of America	1,285,740	13	0
American Nurses' Association	187,000	97	93
National Education Association	1,696,469	75	55

Source: Coalition of Labor Union Women, *Absent from the Agenda: A Report on the Role of Women in American Unions,* 1980, Tables 3 and 5.

period. Nineteenth century working men found their jobs increasingly precarious, as technological change enabled their bosses to replace their skilled labor with new machinery run by women, immigrants, and other (cheaper) labor. Union men decided it was strategically to their advantage to organize only the male workers and to exclude women from the unions, urging them, in fact, to leave the labor force entirely. They reasoned that with the women out, there would be fewer workers left in the labor force (and these would be the male trade unionists), which would force wages upward. In a final bit of miscalculated logic, they thought that since these expelled women could marry trade union men anyway, there was nothing to worry about. Women could just busy themselves tending the hearth and home, spending their husband's wages. Of course, the theory was all wrong. Women were in the labor force because they needed the work and the money to survive. Shunned by the male unions, women remained, for the most part, unorganized with very low pay.

Occasionally, certain trade unions found it useful to accept women members. If they were working in the same trade anyway, women as union members would have to honor union-authorized strikes and union seniority rules. Even when women were admitted to male unions, however, it was usually on an unequal basis; they paid lower dues and received fewer benefits. Women were rarely union officers or organizers; even attending union meetings was impractical or considered unladylike for most women workers. There *were* pioneering female labor leaders, and even strong all-female locals, but they were the exception. Women represented only 4.6% of all union members in 1895, and this dropped to 2.9% in 1908, partly due to the antifemale attitudes of Gompers and the AFL.

Unfortunately, these "dark ages" of the trade union movement continued, even through the trade union growth of the late 1930s and in spite of women's war work and increasing labor force participation. From 1958 to 1973, the proportion of organized women to all women in the labor force dropped from 17% to 12%. True, women were entering the traditionally ununionized sectors of the labor force (white-collar and service work), but the trade union movement was not trying to organize these masses of workers either.

In recent years, the attitudes of the trade union movement seem to have been changing. The president of the AFL-CIO, Lane Kirkland, has spoken out in favor of organizing women and minority workers. Some traditionally male-dominated unions have hired women organizers and toned down their male image. What is going on? Trade unions in America are taking a good look at working women for three reasons: antidiscrimination laws, which apply to unions as well as businesses; the declining membership and power of the trade union movement; and women's own rekindled interest in workplace organizing. Each of these factors is equally complex and critical, and will be examined in turn.

The New Union Welcome: An Obligation Under the Civil Rights Act

One of the biggest shocks to the union movement in recent years was the realization that *they* could be sued by workers for discrimination. Under the provisions of the Equal Pay Act and Title VII of the Civil Rights Act, unions were barred from discriminatory behavior. If a union has over 15 members, it, like any other employer, cannot discriminate in its own staffing decisions. More crucial, though, as a labor organization it cannot exclude, expel, or in any way discriminate against women, nor can it deprive women of their employment opportunities or cause an employer to do so. Correspondingly, unions cannot operate discriminatory training or apprenticeship programs.

Furthermore, according to the courts, unions are bound to act affirmatively to remove the effects of past discrimination in their contracts. It is a violation, then, if a union does not actively oppose unlawful contract provisions that may be currently in effect. Union officials must propose new seniority systems as alternatives to past discriminatory systems. They have to challenge irrelevant "protective" rules that discriminate unfairly against women, such as weight or size qualifications for certain types of jobs. Unions are obligated by law to scrutinize their contracts and demand change in all discriminatory clauses. In addition, they must consider women workers' grievances fully. They can no longer tell women that their problems are not as important as the male workers' complaints.

Already many major unions have begun to take their responsibilities under the Civil Rights Act seriously. The International Union of Electrical, Radio and Machine Workers (IUE), the Communication Workers of America (CWA), and the American Federation of State, County and Municipal Employees (AFSCME) are a few of the major unions that have not only reviewed their collective bargaining contracts, but have even gone to court on behalf of women workers' rights to equal pay for equal work and equal access to all job categories. Legal challenges in 1970 forced unions to give women equal access to apprenticeship programs, perhaps the juiciest plum controlled by the unions, since those 300,000 apprenticeships a year mean access to the highest-paid skilled jobs. But the real battle is shaping up over the question of seniority rules.

Seniority Rules, Layoffs, and Affirmative Action

The trade unions have traditionally considered seniority provisions to be their "number one" victory, the workers' protection against unfair or capricious firings by their bosses. Specific layoff provisions are written into 90% of the major collective bargaining agreements in America, and in 85% of these, seniority is a key factor in determining the order of layoffs. While "last hired, first fired" may have been a brotherly principle for trade unions in the past, it is not the same anymore. Because of past discrimination, women and minorities were not allowed in these unions and therefore could not accrue seniority. Layoffs of those "last hired" just perpetuate the effects of past discrimination; therefore, the seniority system itself can be considered discriminatory.

Many unions, such as the Teamsters and the United Steelworkers, are not giving up their seniority system without a fight, particularly now during recessionary times. Why should male trade unionists get laid off while women and minority workers keep their jobs a little longer? For women and minorities, who only recently have had the chance to work in these jobs after decades of discrimination, it is particularly discouraging to see all the affirmative action struggles of the 1970s washed down the drain in the business slumps of the 1980s.

Whatever the outcome of the legal battles over seniority versus affirmative action hiring, friction between male and female workers has intensified, which only increases business's clout. The EEOC and the academics can discuss "work sharing" (unemployment sharing) and "reverse seniority" schemes, but they cannot solve the basic layoff question. As more plant closures threaten the jobs of even the senior union men (and, indeed, the white collar middle-management employees), there may be more talk about workers' rights to jobs and less argument about who is laid off first. In the meantime, however, the seniority issue is the biggest obstacle to the successful integration of women workers into the trade union movement.

New Blood for a Sagging Union Movement

Antidiscrimination laws have not been the only reason for this new interest in working women from the trade union movement. As mentioned earlier, union membership overall has fallen. In 1976, 20.3% of the labor force was unionized; by 1978, it fell to 19.7%. In 1979 unions won only 46% of their representation elections, one of the smallest percentages in the history of this National Labor Relations Board procedure. Unions are not only losing members certification elections, but their wage contracts are losing ground against the rising cost of living. The image of unionism has been rather tarnished too, with charges of corruption on the one hand and rank-and-file discontent on the other. Unions in America are finally realizing that if they do not grow, they will die.

The drive to revitalize the union movement is focusing on the traditionally unorganized sectors and on the traditionally unorganized in the organized sectors: women and minority workers. Traditionally defined unions, such as the Communication Workers of

America, are expanding their turf by including the retail trades and clerical and service workers. The United Food and Commercial Workers are organizing bank, optical, and pharmaceutical workers. And the traditionally unionized sectors, such as coal mining, are organizing their own women workers these days. In fact, between 1956 and 1976, half of all new union members were women.

Not surprisingly, much of this new interest in unionization has come from women themselves. Women workers have become aware of the higher pay of unionized workers. They have also realized that their protection under antidiscrimination laws is really quite limited. Equal pay laws do not raise the low female wages in all-female occupations, but unions might. Furthermore, taking advantage of legal rights can require a long, expensive, and difficult lawsuit. Union protection, on the other hand, is designed to cover workplace issues. Standard union grievance procedures may be better tailored to on-the-job problems than EEOC procedures. It is not surprising, then, that in spite of the antifemale history of the unions, women workers today are much more interested in unionizing.

Female Power Within the AFL–CIO

The big question is not *whether* to unionize, but *how*. Women can choose to stay within the mainstream, male-dominated labor unions or they can start their own independent unions. As we have seen, the traditional labor movement has tried to appeal more to women workers in recent years. The AFL–CIO, for instance, agreed to support the passage of the Equal Rights Amendment in 1973. In 1974, they sanctioned the establishment of a women's caucus within the AFL–CIO, the Coalition of Labor Union Women (CLUW). The purpose of the CLUW is to press for women's issues within the AFL–CIO. This caucus could become an active force for leadership reform within the AFL–CIO, since it has targeted the absence of women from the upper levels of the AFL–CIO as a major problem for women members. Yet many women wonder if the CLUW is not just an elitist group, divorced from the rank-and-file women workers. Since membership in the coalition is limited to union women, the unorganized and unemployed women are excluded. With such restricted membership, can the CLUW ever speak for the needs of the masses of women workers?

The question of membership eligibility has always been a sore point for women organizers. In 1903, when the National Women's Trade Union League (NWTUL) was formed, the issue of membership was a source of continual friction between the NWTUL and the AFL.

The AFL refused to take the NWTUL seriously, on the grounds that it included working women *and* their "allies"—upper-class feminists who did not have jobs but sympathized with the needs of their working-class sisters. But without these allies, the NWTUL could not have survived: the AFL gave little support, while the wealthy feminists gave their time, energy, and money. The NWTUL organized a lot of women, especially in the early years, even if their eventual decline was due to the lack of a working class sensibility among its upper-class supporters. As one analyst argued:

> *When one section of the leadership has a lot of money and a lot of time to devote to the organization, there is a tendency for those with money and time to become functionaries, to run the office, and to attend the conferences and conventions. As a result, their point of view inevitably predominates. In the case of the NWTUL, this meant a shift in emphasis from organizing women workers to educational and legislative work.* [4]

Isolated from the AFL, the NWTUL developed under the direction of its more bourgeois members, slowly moving away from its original unionizing mission.

The history of the NWTUL is often used as a case in point by the defenders of the CLUW and the AFL–CIO to emphasize the need to keep the women's movement organizations separate from the trade union organizations. Yet many women workers today have found a more constructive approach to the membership question.

Independent Unionization

Recognizing both the historic male domination of the mainstream trade unions and the strength of the women's movement organizations, certain groups of women workers have formed independent organizations of working women. These include the Union Women's Alliance to Gain Equality (Union WAGE), Working Women—National Association of Office Workers, and Women Employed, with local branches such as 9 to 5 and Women Office Workers (WOW). Most of these independent organizations have been formed in the last 10 years, reflecting the strength of the women's movement during this period as well as the real needs of unorganized clerical and office workers. As a 9 to 5 spokesperson explained:

> *For women office workers, the trend toward unionization is clearly on the horizon. But for them to be organized into existing unions in a vacuum—without the context of their rights as women—*

would mean the loss of a potentially vital and progressive force in America's labor movement.[5]

The strength of these organizations can be traced to their inclusive membership policies, their collective/democratic principles, and their creative tactics. Most have rejected the "union members only" policy of organizations backed by the AFL–CIO. Union WAGE, for instance, is open to all working women, including housewives, unemployed workers, retired workers, and women on welfare. Their low dues, cheap newspapers, and anti-elitist operating procedures reinforce their commitment to collective action.

The key to the success of the independents is probably their tactical flexibility. Unlike trade unions, which focus most of their energies on the collective bargaining contract, these women's organizations build their action agendas around locally relevant issues using nonconventional methods. For example, 9 to 5, the Boston office workers branch of Working Women, has developed a broad and active membership because its programs speak to the needs of workers in that particular area. Activists in 9 to 5 realized that clerical wages in their area were artificially low when they discovered the Boston Survey Group:

... a consortium of Boston's 40 largest companies, whose members conduct a semi-annual clerical salary survey that contributes to depressing the wages of office workers.[6]

They mounted a campaign against the Boston Survey Group, publicly demanding that key employers resign from this group and asking the Federal Trade Commission to investigate antitrust aspects of their activities. Since the Boston Federal Reserve Bank plays a key role in this employer's association, women in 9 to 5 demanded access, under the Freedom of Information Act, to the Fed's records. The campaign has already achieved the resignation of one powerful bank from the group; 9 to 5 members have continued to apply pressure on the other members. Similarly, a subgroup of 9 to 5, Women in Publishing (WIP), has tried to help women in publishing by setting up a "Resource Bank," with information on wages and promotion policies of major Boston-area publishers.

On the streets, these groups pass out leaflets, hold demonstrations, and engage in "street theater" actions. Recently, for instance, a 9 to 5 group awarded a "grey wig" to an employer known for age discrimination; other units have offered "pettiest boss in town" awards to infamous offenders.[7] They often finance their groups by combining fundraising and social activities, such as running bake sales and giving benefit showings of films such as *9 to 5*.

Union WAGE, a group based on the West Coast, mobilizes support for striking women and lends assistance to women who want to organize a union. Their Household Worker Rights Project recently assisted a group of over 2,000 household workers in San Diego, the United Domestic Workers, to sign the first union contract for household workers.[8] They have lent key support to a wide range of women's organizing campaigns, including the 1980 hotel workers strike in San Francisco and various clerical workers' strikes in California. Most of these working women's organizations provide information to workers about their job rights, fight against discrimination, help to organize unorganized workers, and publicize occupational health and safety needs.

How do these independent organizations relate to the traditional trade union movement? As a 9 to 5 member explained:

9 to 5 activists serve both to stimulate union interest among women and build a large group of women workers that will have an impact on those unions.[9]

Recently, a major AFL–CIO union, the Service Employees International Union, joined forces with Working Women to form District 925 (from 9 to 5) to organize clerical workers on a national basis. The president of the Service Employees explained that District 925 would be run "for women and by women who understand their problems."[10] It may be the first time in history that a major AFL–CIO union leader has recognized the need for a female-run and female-dominated union. This landmark achievement is a tribute to the independents; for it is they who have proven the real need for women-oriented unions and demonstrated their ability to organize effectively.

The moral of this story should be clear. Unions have not emerged from their "dark ages" voluntarily. It has taken lawsuits to remind them that they cannot discriminate against women. They have had to watch their power deteriorate as they refused to go out and organize women workers. Even more importantly, however, they have needed a big push from the women's movement to make them realize what women workers really want—higher wages, better fringe benefits, and more. As women strikers said in 1912, "We want bread and roses."

Additional Readings

For a solid history of trade union women in America, try B. Wertheimer's *We Were There: The Story of Working Women in America* (Pantheon, 1977). Other books cover more specialized areas of interest. For example, J. Tepperman's *Not Servants, Not Machines* (Beacon Press, 1976) is a good study of women office workers and the unionization struggle. For a somewhat old, but still very relevant examination of the union seniority versus affirmative action dilemma, see "Last Hired, First Fired—Layoffs and Civil Rights," Report of the U.S. Commission on Civil Rights, February 1977. For a look at unionism from the dissident women's point of view, see J. Maupin, *Working Women and their Organizations* (Union WAGE Education Committee, 1974). Occasionally, the *Monthly Labor Review* will have an "update" article on the participation of women in trade unions, providing current statistics on membership trends.

Notes

1. Coalition of Labor Union Women (CLUW), *Absent from the Agenda: A Report on the Role of Women in American Unions,* 1980, Table 1.

2. J. Maupin, *Working Women and Their Organizations,* (Union WAGE Education Committee, 1974), p. 21.

3. L. Le Grande, "Women in Labor Organizations: Their Ranks are Increasing," *Monthly Labor Review,* August 1978, p. 10.

4. J. Maupin, p. 23.

5. C. Samuels, *The Forgotten Five Millions: Women in Public Employment,* p. 262.

6. *9 to 5 News,* Vol. 10, #1, February/March 1981, p. 1.

7. "Rebellion Behind the Typewriter," *Business Week,* April 28, 1980, p. 85.

8. *Union WAGE,* January/February 1981.

9. C. Samuels, p. 263.

10. "Women's Group Set to Organize Office Workers," *New York Times,* 3/4/81.

Is It Better Elsewhere?

To ask whether women's position is better in other countries raises difficult and perhaps unanswerable questions. It is hard to select the criterion by which "better" should be judged. Look at Table 11-1, which summarizes some recent statistics on women's fertility, marriage rates, life expectancy, labor force participation rates, urbanization, and literacy in various countries of the world. How can this data be interpreted? For example, is women's position best in countries where the ratio of female to male life expectancy is highest? This index would suggest that the women of Hong Kong (female/male life expectancy: 74/68) are in a better position than the women of Iceland (79/73), which ignores absolute female longevity differences, as well as the differential status of widowhood in the two cultures. Perhaps Icelandic widows lead a more satisfying life than widows in Hong Kong.

Let us try another sample statistic. Some would argue that the labor force participation rate of women is the best indicator of women's advancement, so women in Barbados (40% of the labor force) enjoy a higher status than women in Germany or France (36% of the labor force). This indicator would suggest, however, that there is something inherently preferable in labor force work or that higher status can be derived from labor force participation, two very debatable hypotheses.

Alternatively, consult Table 11-2, which goes beyond labor force participation rates and shows the sectoral distribution of women

TABLE 11-1
Indicators of Women's Status Worldwide

Region or Country	Total Fertility Rate (per woman)[1]	Percentage of Married Women 15–19[2]	Life Expectancy at Birth: Male/Female (years)[3]	Women as a Percentage of Total Labor Force: 1980[4]	Employed Women in Agriculture: 1975 (percent)[5]	Percentage of Urban Dwellers, 1975: Male/Female[6]	Percent Enrolled in School, 1975: Ages 6–11, Male/Female[7]	Percent Enrolled in School, 1975: Ages 12–17, Male/Female[7]	Percentage of Literate Adults, Male/Female[8]
WORLD	3.8	30	56/59	35	49	39/40	76/64	55/46	67/54
More developed	2.0	8	68/76	40	13	67/68	94/94	84/85	98/97
Less developed	4.4	39	54/56	33	70	28/28	70/53	42/28	52/32
AFRICA	6.4	44	47/50	32	73	26/25	59/43	39/24	33/15
Northern Africa	6.2	34	53/55	9	43	40/40	70/45	42/23	44/18
Western Africa	6.8	70	45/48	40	62	20/19	44/30	29/16	20/6
Middle Africa	6.0	49	44/47	37	92	31/28	78/54	52/26	35/9
Eastern Africa	6.6	32	46/49	35	87	14/12	52/41	33/20	29/14
EAST ASIA	2.3	2	63/67	38	66	31/30	99/99	85/80	97/92
China, People's Rep. of	2.3	—	62/66	38	73	24/23	—	—	—
Hong Kong	2.6	3	68/74	34	2	90/90	89/89	83/79	90/64
Japan	1.8	1	73/77	40	18	75	100/100	95/95	99/97

CARIBBEAN	3.8	19	61/65	30	28	47/50	85/87	60/59	67/66
Bahamas	3.5	10	67/71	—	—	21/26	—	—	90/89
Barbados	2.2	16	68/72	40	16	36/39	—	—	98/98
Cuba	2.5	28	70/74	21	12	61/65	100/100	67/63	76/80
Dominica	—	—	65/70	—	—	36/39	—	—	58/61
Dominican Republic	5.4	22	58/62	12	9	44/48	75/79	56/56	69/66
Grenada	—	—	65/70	47	58	36/39	—	—	77/76
Haiti	5.9	5	49/52	38	4	20/24	44/34	23/16	29/18
Jamaica	3.7	23	68/72	—	—	44/47	90/58	58/65	79/85
Netherland Antilles	3.1	—	67/71	—	—	21/26	—	—	93/92
Puerto Rico	2.4	9	70/76	29	—	64/66	100/100	89/94	89/87
EUROPE	2.0	7	69/75	37	20	66/67	95/96	81/80	96/93
Northern Europe	1.8	9	70/76	37	3	82/84	98/98	82/83	99/99
Denmark	1.7	2	71/77	38	7	80/84	99/99	37/76	99
Finland	1.7	4	68/76	42	1	55/58	86/90	82/87	100
Iceland	2.3	3	73/79	30	6	85/88	—	—	—
Ireland	3.4	2	70/75	28	6	52/57	96/97	81/85	98
Norway	1.8	5	72/78	29	9	46/49	84/84	88/89	99
Sweden	1.7	1	72/78	38	5	83/86	80/82	86/87	99
United Kingdom	1.7	11	69/75	38	1	89/90	98/98	85/85	99
Western Europe	1.6	5	69/76	35	6	75/77	95/96	87/89	98/98
Austria	1.6	6	68/75	40	12	51/54	93/93	70/72	99
Belgium	1.7	7	68/75	31	2	71/72	97/97	85/87	97/97
France	1.9	5	69/77	36	8	74/76	97/100	79/85	97/97
Germany, Fed. Rep. of	1.4	6	69/75	36	5	82/84	96/96	90/93	99
Luxembourg	1.5	6	68/75	27	1	73/74	97/98	78/71	100
Netherlands	1.6	4	72/78	26	1	76/77	92/94	90/88	100
Switzerland	1.5	4	72/78	34	6	55/57	82/84	74/65	100

(continued)

TABLE 11-1
(continued)

Region or Country	Total Fertility Rate (per woman)[1]	Percentage of Married Women 15–19[2]	Life Expectancy at Birth: Male/Female (years)[3]	Women as a Percentage of Total Labor Force: 1980[4]	Employed Women in Agriculture: 1975 (percent)[5]	Percentage of Urban Dwellers, 1975: Male/Female[6]	Percent Enrolled in School, 1975: Ages 6–11, Male/Female[7]	Percent Enrolled in School, 1975: Ages 12–17, Male/Female[7]	Percentage of Literate Adults, Male/Female[8]
Eastern Europe	2.3	9	68/74	45	36	56/57	92/91	80/81	97/92
Bulgaria	2.3	—	69/75	43	56	59/58	77/78	80/80	96/86
Czechoslovakia	2.4	8	67/74	45	10	58/60	95/98	65/73	—
German Democratic Rep.	1.8	6	69/75	46	10	75/76	99/100	84/84	—
Hungary	2.2	15	67/73	42	14	49/51	96/97	77/71	98/98
Poland	2.3	4	67/75	46	40	53/55	90/87	73/78	99/97
Romania	2.6	21	68/73	45	69	45/44	89/84	99/95	94/84
Southern Europe	2.3	7	69/74	29	28	56/56	97/97	73/66	93/85
Albania	4.2	—	68/71	40	78	37/33	—	—	80/63
Greece	2.3	11	71/75	33	62	57/57	100/99	76/64	93/76
Italy	1.9	6	70/76	29	14	66/68	100/100	77/70	95/93
Malta	2.0	3	69/73	22	7	81/81	95/97	80/72	—
Portugal	2.5	5	66/72	26	24	27/29	98/97	57/54	78/65
Spain	2.6	3	70/76	22	11	70/71	100/100	67/61	94/86
Yugoslavia	2.2	3	67/72	36	48	38/39	69/70	90/79	92/76

	2.4	10	63/74	49	15	61/61	99/99	77/82	100/100
USSR									
NORTH AMERICA	1.8	11	69/77	38	1	71/73	99/99	95/95	99/99
Canada	1.9	7	70/77	34	2	77/79	100/100	89/90	98/98
United States	1.8	11	69/77	38	0.4	71/72	99/99	95/96	99/99

[1] The total fertility rate (TFR) of a given year indicates the average number of children that would be born to a woman during her lifetime if she were to have children throughout her childbearing years (usually considered ages 15 to 49) at the same rate as women of those ages did in that year. It is a good measure of the current level of childbearing in a particular country or region. Most TFRs shown here refer to the 1975–80 period and are from the UN 1978 Assessment. Other sources were: U.S. Bureau of the Census, A Compilation of Age-Specific Fertility Rates for Developing Countries, International Research Document No. 7, Washington, D.C., December 1979; and Country Reports of the World Fertility Survey.

[2] Data are from the most recent census or survey available and generally refer to some point in the 1970s. Sources were: unpublished table of census and survey data compiled by Leela Visaria of the Population Reference Bureau; and Population Information Program, The Johns Hopkins University, "Age at Marriage and Fertility," Population Reports, Series M, No. 4, prepared by Alice Henry and Phyllis T. Piotrow, Baltimore, Md., November 1979.

[3] Average number of years a newborn child could be expected to live if current mortality conditions were to continue throughout his or her lifetime. Data refer to the 1975–80 period and are from the UN 1978 Assessment. Estimates of life expectancy for most less developed countries should be regarded as rough approximations only.

[4] Projections from ILO, Labour Force Estimates and Projections. . . .

[5] Extrapolations of ILO projections (ILO, Labour Force Estimates and Projections . . .) by Amy Ong Tsui and Donald J. Bogue in "Declining World Fertility: Trends, Causes, Implications," Popula-Bulletin, Vol. 33, No. 4, October 1978.

[6] The percentage of males and females living in areas defined as urban by each country. Data are from UN, Population Division, Age-Sex Distributions in Rural and Urban Areas, ESA/P/WP.64, New York, September 1979.

[7] Percent of males and females in each age group enrolled in school. Data are from unpublished tables of the Office of Statistics, UNESCO, Paris.

[8] Country definitions of "adults" and "literacy" vary. These data are generally based on the most recent census or survey from which an estimate can be derived and come from UNESCO, Statistical Yearbook 1977.

Source: The World's Women Data Sheet.

TABLE 11-2
Percentage of Women in the Total Labor Force in Seven Occupational Groups

Country	Year	Professional, Technical, and Related Workers	Administrative, Executive, and Managerial Workers	Clerical Workers	Sales Workers	Crafts and Production Workers	Service Workers	Farmers and Fishermen
Austria	1975		43.7[a]		56.7	16.9	68.7	48.2
Australia	1971	42.3	12.0	63.8	48.3	13.4	62.7	15.5
Canada	1976	48.2	20.2	74.6	34.5	12.2	50.5	18.6
Finland	1975	45.0	17.9	82.3	55.3	24.3	83.8	44.9
Germany, West	1970	34.3	13.5	54.6	52.7	17.3	54.6	48.1
Israel	1975	50.3	7.4	55.4	28.6	10.8	52.3	20.1
Japan	1975	38.4	5.3	49.6	39.3	24.0	53.5	49.3
Romania	1966	44.4	40.5		40.7	17.7	48.6	58.6
Sweden	1975	48.1	11.3	78.4	47.6	17.4	78.0	24.3
United Kingdom	1971	38.3	8.4	60.3	47.4	17.1	69.3	13.1
United States	1975	41.6	19.7	78.1	43.5	17.9	62.3	15.9

[a]Combined percentage for the first three occupational groups.

Source: International Labor Organization, *Yearbook of Labor Statistics,* 1976. Published in A. Cook, *The Working Mother: A Survey of Problems and Programs in Nine Countries,* p. 11.

workers in various countries. Should we argue that women's position is higher in those countries where women form the largest proportion of the professional/technical workforce? By this criteria, Israeli women, who form 50.3% of all professional and technical workers, must enjoy a higher status than British women, who make up only 38.3% of the professional workers. But this argument assumes that professional work enjoys high status in every culture; a look at Table 11-3 reveals that this is by no means true everywhere. Table 11-3 shows the distribution of women workers in various economic sectors in the Soviet Union. There, construction, transport, and industrial

TABLE 11-3
Distribution of Soviet Women Workers and Average Monthly Earnings, by Economic Sector, 1975

Economic Sector	Number of Women Workers and Employees	Women as Percentage of the Labor Force	Average Monthly Earnings (Rubles)
Construction	3,002,000	28	176.8
Transport	2,211,000	24	173.5
Industry (production personnel)	1,662,000	49	162.0
Science and scientific services	2,015,000	50	155.4
Nationwide average	52,539,000	51	145.8
Credit and state insurance	423,000	82	133.8
Apparatus of government and economic administration	1,457,000	65	130.6
Education	5,904,000	73	126.9
Agriculture	4,530,000	44	126.8
Communications	1,042,000	68	123.6
Housing and municipal economy, everyday services	2,010,000	53	109.0
Trade, public catering, materials and equipment, supply and sales	6,763,000	76	108.7
Arts	207,000	47	103.1
Public health, physical culture, social welfare	4,851,000	84	102.3
Culture	747,000	73	92.2

Source: Calculated from figures given in Tsentral'noe statisticheskoe upravlenie, Narodnoe khoziaistvo SSSR v 1975 g. (Moscow, 1976), pp. 542–43; 546–47, in G. Lapidus, Women in Soviet Society, p. 192.

production workers all earn more than scientific, cultural, or health workers, which presumably indicates their status differential as well.

It is difficult enough to select appropriate indices of women's position relative to men in any given country; it seems impossible to find indicators that are cross-culturally valid. In spite of these difficulties, some experts have recently devised what they call a "Physical Quality of Life Index" (PQLI)—an average of life expectancy, infant mortality, and literacy rates for various countries. This PQLI cannot be used to answer *broad* questions of women's status or progress, but it may become a useful indicator of certain physical aspects of the quality of life worldwide.

The Problem of Identifying the Dynamics of Women's Progress

Unfortunately, these status indicators yield a very static picture of women's positions. It may not be that important to know that 80% of Cuban women are literate, compared to 99% of Northern European women; it may be *more* important to realize the relative speed with which Cuban women have attained their literacy. In fact, the rate of change of a social indicator may be more critical than its absolute level or its level relative to levels in other countries. The *dynamics* of change in women's positions are more crucial than static comparisons of status; we need to identify the factors that contribute to the improvement of women's positions. This will be ultimately more useful than statistics about women's status elsewhere.

Is Birth Control Really the Answer?

The search for clues to the dynamics of women's advancement, however, is not straightforward. Many solutions have been proposed and implemented, only to be found unsatisfactory. For a while, birth control was the proposed panacea for women's inferior status, particularly for women in the heavily-populated, third-world countries. International agencies and, more importantly, international drug companies, sold birth control pills and devices to the women of these nations, with the promise that these products would solve their problems. Without children, these women were told, their standard of living would improve; they could enter the paid labor force and earn their way to emancipation. Some women who used these birth control products went to an early grave instead, a rather macabre "liberation." Others found that without children, they lost their social status, their financial security for their old age, or their entire sense of community, their *raison d'être*. For example, a study of Indian peasant families concluded:

> *Peasants felt that having large families was not the cause of their poverty; indeed, many children could be a solution to their poverty, since children ... could help them work the land or send back remittances from city jobs.*[1]

Population control programs are certainly no "quick fix" to the problems of women's progress, and they often create more difficulties than they solve. According to the planners, the use of birth control pills would enable the women of third-world countries to enter the paid labor force and become "productive workers." Yet for many of these women, paid work can be obtained only by migrating from the rural to the urban areas, where they can work as domestic servants or factory workers at subsistence wages. This scenario serves the interests of their prospective employers; indeed, some employers distribute birth control pills routinely to all their women workers.[2] Yet it should not be surprising that many third-world women do not consider this "emancipation" at all.

Does Industrialization Help Women?

This second panacea—industrialization—has been suggested to third-world women, too, although its impact on men is characteristically quite different from its impact on women. Since in many parts of the world it is the women who work traditionally in agriculture and commerce, industrialization efforts can sabotage the structure of women's role by not substituting a comparably productive way of life. For example, as slash-and-burn agricultural styles are modernized by the introduction of the plough, women's labor is displaced:

> *The advent of the plough usually entails a radical shift in sex roles in agriculture; men take over the ploughing even in regions where the hoeing had formerly been women's work. At the same time, the amount of weeding to be done by women may decline on land*

ploughed before sowing and planting, and either men or women may get a new job of collecting feed for the animals and feeding them.[3]

Women are usually displaced in the modernization process either because the foreign experts train the men in the new techniques or because the men are given control of the relatively expensive equipment and the newly apportioned land.

In many Southeast Asian countries, planners are just not interested in whether rural women retain their agricultural roles. Instead, their idea is to insert these women into the labor forces assembled for the multinational firms that have recently set up factories in these countries. According to conservative estimates, there are already 2 million third-world women industrial workers.[4] The young women of the third world are a bonanza for the electronics, semiconductor, and clothing firms, since their wages are very low: the 1976 average wage for unskilled women in Hong Kong was 55¢ an hour; in South Korea, 52¢ an hour; in the Philippines, 32¢ an hour; and in Indonesia, 17¢ an hour.[5] In many cases, these wages are less than the cost of living at a subsistence level in those countries. For instance, at a U.S. firm's electronics plant in the Philippines, wages for women range from $34 to $46 per month, yet the minimum cost of living there is estimated at $37 per month.[6]

How do these workers survive? Most of the multinational firms have built dormitories with their factories. The girls sleep in shifts and eat sparsely. In the eyes of their employers, girls are ideal workers because they are cheap and obedient. As a personnel manager in a Taiwan factory commented:

"Young male workers are too restless and impatient to do monotonous work with no career value. If displeased, they sabotage the machines and even threaten the foreman. But girls? At most they cry a little . . . ."[7]

Working conditions are so rough for these women that some have tried to unionize, in spite of the threat of dismissal they face if discovered. In many areas, women have resorted to more creative tactics for achieving improvements. According to reports, Malaysian women, for example, have tried mass hysteria in their factories as a form of "covert industrial conflict."[8] Typically, a worker may scream that she sees apparitions in her microscope, and in seconds, all the other women may start shrieking as well. As the *Wall Street Journal* commented:

Mass hysteria doesn't increase productivity. To let the dust settle, factories have closed for a week or more. And as modern manufacturers continue setting up in Malaysia—hysteria doesn't seem to have shaken up anybody's plans—outbreaks of hysteria apparently are proliferating. Fifty cases made the news in the 1970s, but an academic here calls that "merely suggestive" of the actual number. An ill-starred shoe factory in Malacca has had 40 episodes in two years. "Every other night," says a factory manager in Seremban, his men drag a victim from the floor before her delirium becomes infectious.[9]

All of these hysterical episodes may not be deliberate attempts to avoid work. Some may be due to the fumes from hazardous chemicals in the workplace, since in many electronics factories the circuits are dipped into open vats of acid as part of the production process.[10] There is little regulation of health hazards in these factories; women electronics workers routinely lose their eyesight from strain, if not from the chemical fumes. Work in such subhuman conditions cannot be considered emancipatory, even if it moves women out of their rural subsistence lifestyles.

Does Modernization Help Women?

While many experts have learned to question birth control and mass industrialization as "solutions" to improving women's position, they still try to promote the "modernization" panacea: remove the forces of traditional culture, particularly religion, and women will be emancipated. It is traditional culture, according to these usually ethnocentric experts, that oppresses women. Wipe out the backward elements of traditional culture and women can have an equal chance for advancement.

While many feminists agree that aspects of certain traditional cultures (such as veiling the face of women or the genital mutilation of girls in strict Muslim countries) are oppressive, they are usually careful in their condemnation of other women's traditional cultures. The blanket suppression of tradition in favor of modern, Western culture is not only morally questionable, but may entail many more practical hardships for the women involved. If Westernization removes women from their traditional economic bases, in agriculture or in trade, and instead promotes urbanization and cash-crop agriculture for foreign-dominated commerce, women can end up more dependent than ever before on men for their access to newly important cash incomes. As a young Kenyan woman told her interviewer:

> *Life is much more difficult now because everybody is dependent on money. Long ago, money was unheard of. No one needed money. But now you can't even get food without cash....*[11]

Yet it is only the men who are mobile enough to migrate to areas where they can earn cash. The women maintain the household as best they can, and "all too frequently neither the cash nor the men get back to the families."[12]

A More Holistic Approach to Women's Progress

If birth control, industrialization, and modernization are all panaceas and not the real agents for the improvement of women's condition, what are? What does determine improvement in women's status? The answer is obviously complex, but must relate to the totality of the society, the culture in which the women live. This is not meant to be a statement of pure cultural relativism, but rather a rejection of the implicit cultural imperialism of the simplistic approaches usually offered. Rejecting panaceas, we need to examine larger frameworks. Specifically, we need to identify the type of commitment a country's economic system makes to the advancement of women. Since different economic systems view the "woman problem" in different terms, their approaches to policy toward women differ in structure and results. The first task, then, is to identify the different approaches of the various types of economic systems to the woman question.

Laissez Faire Economies and Women

On the extreme laissez faire end of the spectrum, we find the "free enterprise" economies, such as that in the United States and in other capitalist countries. Here the approach to the woman question is the same as the approach to any other subgroup of the population: the "free market" is sex blind. According to the laissez faire ideology, women can enter the market, like anyone else, and the market will recompense them fairly, according to their productivity. They can use that compensation, that wage, for instance, to purchase whatever goods they desire. The free market is indifferent as to whether males or females are hired, or how those people spend their incomes.

The only sense in which a "women's policy" can be justified, according to the free enterprise system, is if there are impediments to the operation of this free market. If men use their power to restrict women to certain jobs, or to pay women less than their productivity warrants, then intervention to restore markets to perfect competition is permissible. Such extreme faith in the justice and efficiency of the free market is seldom actually heard, but this is the philosophical basis of laissez faire economies. The realities are actually different, as we have seen.

Social Democratic Economies and Women

To the left on the political spectrum are the social democratic economies, which endorse state intervention in markets to achieve socially desirable goals. When Sweden decided, for instance, that sexual inequality was socially undesirable and that intervention in labor market policy was necessary, a social consensus on this approach led to its implementation as law, above the market forces.

Social democratic systems obviously do not believe that the free market is the best indicator of social desires: in these systems, electoral votes override dollar votes. Given this orientation, policies on the women question can run the full gamut of whatever the citizens choose to include in their legislation, from "parent leave" for child rearing to public subsidization of community laundries. Home help services, for example, were approved by the Swedish legislature in 1943; today, they employ 1% of the total labor force. Under this system, the home help service sends out helpers to assist people with their housekeeping, child care, or care of the infirm. The service is available to all Swedish people, not just the low-income people, although there is a sliding scale of fees.[13] This service is only one example of the many types of social programs sponsored by the Swedish government in response to a popular vote. Thus, social democratic governments are interventionistic (since they do not try to leave everything to the private sector). Yet they are still market economies.

Socialist Economies and Women

Looking toward the other end of the economic spectrum, we can take a look at the nonmarket, socialist systems. In Soviet-style socialism, the first stage is the revolution of the working class against the factory and land owners. After the successful revolution, the workers' state consolidates this victory and plans social production in the interests of all working people. The woman question is a second-order concern for two reasons. First, according to socialist theory, women's oppression is a structural feature of capitalist exploitation, a way of pitting male workers against female workers and exploiting them further. So only the working class revolution, by removing capitalist exploitation, can remove women's oppression. Second, any "woman's problem" that remains after the revolution is only residual and should be dealt with by bringing women out of the private home and into social production, where women can develop a socialist consciousness. Thus Soviet feminists, such as Alexandra Kollontai, set up children's centers and worker restaurants to free women from their prerevolutionary housework and child care duties, enabling them to work in Soviet factories. The Soviet feminists also reminded their comrades that male chauvinism was unacceptable in the new workers' state, but none of these efforts really got off the ground. Unfortunately, the Soviet leadership decided that there was a trade-off between the women's demands and the need for rapid economic development in the new Soviet workers' state. These "costly" women's ideas would have to wait; first, the state needed women's factory labor, women's high birth rates, and women's cheap housework. They could afford these expensive women's programs only later on. Soviet women have had to bear the cost of this "trade-off" philosophy.

Referring back to Table 11-3 (see page 181), we can see that women in the Soviet Union are more heavily concentrated in the lower-paying sectors of the Soviet economy, such as in education, trade, public health and welfare, and cultural work. As indicated in Table 11-4, which shows the allocation of time by males and females in the Soviet Union, the double burden for Soviet women has not disappeared either. Soviet women spend as much time as men on their jobs, but they spend over twice as much time as the men on housework, leaving them much less free time. As one (irate) Soviet woman recently wrote:

Although women are now legally equal to men, male psychology has not changed. For many women, marriage means a working day equal to a man's, plus another working day at home. Men seldom view marriage as a joint venture. A man I know is a good example. When he married, he couldt't boil water and he felt imposed upon if his wife asked him to go to the bakery. After his divorce, he lived alone and became a wonderful cook and housekeeper. But when he remarried he reverted completely to type.[14]

TABLE 11-4
A Comparison of Time Budgets of Male and Female Workers in the Soviet Union

Time-Budget Categories	Percentage of Week Devoted to Given Activity		Ratio of Time Spent by Females in Given Category to that of Males
	Males	Females	
Working time			
Low	28	27	
High	32	31	
Average	30	29	.96
Physiological needs			
Low	38	37	
High	42	40	
Average	41	39	.95
Housework			
Low	5	11	
High	10	22	
Average	8	19	2.37
Free time			
Low	16	9	
High	25	17	
Average	21	13	.62

Note: The table was compiled by transforming the data presented in the above studies into percentages of time in a seven-day week in the interest of standardization. In the Soviet usage, "working time" includes both actual work and time connected with work, as in travel; "physiological needs" include eating, sleeping, and self-care; "housework" includes shopping, food preparation, care of the household and possessions, and direct physical care of young children; "free time" includes hobbies, public activities, activities with children, study, and various forms of amusement and rest.

Sources: L. A. Gordon and E. V. Klopov, *Chelovek posle raboty* (Moscow, 1972); V. D. Patrushev, *Vremia kak ekonomicheskaia kategoriia* (Moscow, 1966); G. S. Petrosian, *Vnerabochee vremia trudiashchikhsia* (Novosibirsk, 1961); V. A. Artemov, V. I. Bolgov, and O. V. Volskaia, *Statistika biudzhetov vremeni trudiashchikhsia* (Moscow, 1967); G. V. Osipov and S. F. Frolov, "Vnerabochee vremya i ego ispol'zovanie," in G. V. Osipov, ed., *Sotsiologiia v SSSR*, Vol. 2 (Moscow, 1965). Published in G. Lapidus, *Women in Soviet Society*, p. 271.

It is not only male attitudes that keep Soviet women burdened with housework. Improved living standards and an increasing emphasis on the family sphere have compounded the problem. Soviet women, like their Western sisters, are also facing the problem of rising quality standards in housework. This Soviet woman's remarks could have been made by the average American woman:

> *Yes, a washing machine frees me from heavy physical work . . . but now if there is the slightest spot on the linen I toss it into the washing machine. But after all, the washing machine doesn't iron.*

*The time that I formerly spent washing clothes I now spend ironing.
If there had not been a washing machine in the house I would not
so quickly toss the linen into the wash-basin. Everyday appliances
free the housewife from heavy physical strains—shaking out rugs,
washing clothing, heating and carrying water, but the time it takes
to carry out all the household tasks has remained the same as it
used to be.*[15]

Clearly, removing the double burden requires more than a socialist
revolution (and more than better vacuum cleaners).

Communist Economies and Women

As a final study, we can consider the communist type of economic
system, as found in Maoist China, for example. In this type of system,
after the successful revolution against capitalist exploitation, the
workers' state constructs a new definition of economic development.
Economic development and growth are seen only in terms of the
advancement of the people themselves. Society is richer, for example,
if diseases are reduced or if literacy becomes widespread. The
"woman question" thus takes on a new dimension; the advancement
of women and economic growth are—for the first time—seen as
complementary goals. Unlike in other economic systems, where
women's advancement is considered part of a "trade-off," in the
Chinese system women are part of the meaning of progress or development. Women's labor is productive and productivity or growth is
viewed as having little meaning if half the population is left behind.

What has this meant for Chinese women? Most important,
Chinese women took the leadership in defining their needs in the
new society. Child care was necessary, they said, not just to allow
women to participate in social production, but also to educate young
children in socially responsible directions. As one writer put it, "To
liberate the mother from the child is first of all to liberate the child."[16]
Taking children seriously, as the future builders of society, implies
that child-care centers are responsible for developing the child's
sense of social responsibility and usefulness.

Child care was probably not as difficult a problem in China as
housework. How could Chinese women take part in social production
and political work if they still had to do hours of housework every
night? Housework in less developed countries such as China con-
sumes many hours of hard labor—fetching water, grinding grain,
gathering fuel, and making shoes and clothes, in addition to the usual
washing, cleaning, and cooking. Mechanization of housework was no

answer, since household appliances had not freed Western women and would only use up scarce resources needed for other sectors of the economy. As Mao said, "To liberate women is not to manufacture washing machines."[17]

· What did the Chinese try instead? The basic theme of their efforts was to remove housework from the private home, since Chinese women had already found out that their husbands would *speak* of sharing but never *do* much housework. So housework was transplanted into the public sector through the institution of community service centers, which were collective enterprises set up by local residents. A single service center might have dining facilities, nursery schools, sewing centers, recreational facilities, bath houses—whatever local people wanted:

> *They sold consumer goods, books and newspapers, received savings deposits for the bank, repaired furniture and household utensils, washed and mended clothing, did housework and performed a hundred and one other services. Women returned home from work to find hot meals locally available and their homes neatly cleaned. There were nurseries where mothers might leave their babies for a few hours to go shopping, see a film or go to spare-time school.... When a working housewife went to work in the morning, she could entrust all her domestic jobs for the day to the service centre by leaving a note in the box on the door. Such services might include shopping, booking train tickets, mailing letters, drawing savings from the bank, mending furniture and utensils, sending clothes to the laundry and cleaning and decorating homes.*[18]

A service center in Peking was described as follows:

> *Both big and small affairs are handled quickly and efficiently by its staff of eight housewives and two elderly men. A middle-aged woman drops in to rest her feet and have a cup of hot water between shopping errands. An old woman asks for help in writing a letter to her daughter in another province. A housewife brings a bundle of socks and children's clothes for washing and mending. A newly married couple asks for help in cleaning and moving into their new apartment. A boy wants a ticket for the evening show at the local cinema. A man wants to call a taxi to take his pregnant wife to the hospital....*[19]

It is true that the ideological reformation was never completed and women were still associated with this collective provision of household services. Yet the service workshop system relieved individual women of this burden and represented a major step toward erasing the notion of housework as a wife's duty. Chinese ideological campaigns strengthened this move by emphasizing that each person—even the young child—is responsible for his or her own care. Chinese women were not to accept the role of "personal servant" anymore. Apart from the particular programs, the philosophy of the social system is progressive: their planners realize that Chinese growth means the progress of Chinese women, and that these women can design the projects they need for their development.

How Different Systems Treat Women's Triple Burden

Looking back over these different economic systems, it is interesting that women worldwide seem to be faced with similar issues: combining housework, child care, and paid labor market work. Furthermore, each type of economic system structures women's options according to its interests. Consider the childbearing question, for example. All economic systems rely on women to produce a labor force, yet each system has slightly different ways of providing incentives for women to bear different numbers of children. The free enterprise economies break with principle and use the legal system to impose business's preferences on women. Ironically, the same free enterprise conservatives who fight government intervention in markets try to use the government's legal system to deny women reproductive freedom—the choice of whether or not to bear children. The interventionistic social democracies are more consistent. They set targets for ideal population policy and use financial incentives to encourage women to comply. The Soviet socialists seem to have a new problem convincing women to have children in the appropriate fashion, as the data on rising illegitimacy in Table 11-5 suggest.

While illegitimate children now number one out of every 10 live births in the Soviet Union, bearing these children is apparently the choice of older women who are looking for a source of satisfaction in their mature years.[20]

For a society to take a progressive approach to women's fertility decisions, it must do more than just remove the social handicaps of childbearing women, unburdening them of the financial and time costs involved. It must also consider women's rights to determine their own needs on this question. The same criteria apply to women's market work. In addition to removing obstacles for women in social

TABLE 11-5
Illegitimate Births per Thousand Unmarried Women,
Belorussia: 1959 and 1970

Age Group	1959	1970
15–19	2.7	7.1
20–24	16.3	73.9
25–29	36.8	98.1
30–34	39.1	87.2
35–39	27.1	47.2

Source: Larisa Kuznetsova, "Obeshchal zhenitsa," *Literaturnaia gazeta,* April 14, 1973, p. 12. Published in G. Lapidus, *Women in Soviet Society,* p. 259.

production, a progressive society must recognize women's role: the determination of policy. In fact, the key to successful dynamics on the "woman question" lies in women's leadership in determining that policy. This has been the historic function of women's movements worldwide—in the United States, in China, in Cuba, in France, all over. Women's movements do not always develop "correct" or "successful" positions, but they are the right *vehicles* for developing those strategies.

Conclusions

Is the position of women better elsewhere? Although this question remains unanswered, we at least have a more useful way to approach the issues than comparing labor force participation rates or fertility rates. Looking beyond the yearly statistics, one must examine the approach of the whole economic system to women's advancement in order to evaluate their programs and prospects. A noted scholar of women's work summarized the issues succinctly when she wrote:

In the West in the name of freedom and individual choice—matters of high valence—individual women who "wish to go to work" are left to solve all the problems of finding jobs, providing child care, and maintaining the home at an acceptable standard on their own.[21]

In socialist countries, she continued:

. . . it is accepted that women should and will work and that if they are to work at maximum efficiency they will need help with arrangements for child care and for assistance with housework.[22]

Furthermore, we have examined the more progressive position, which sees women's advancement as part and parcel of total social advancement.

Finally, it is not enough for the social system to have a progressive conception of the value of women's emancipation. The determination of the meaning of emancipation must be in the hands of women themselves.

Additional Readings

There are so many good sources on women's positions in other countries that it is difficult to choose just a few. For statistical comparisons, A. Cook's *The Working Mother: A Survey of Problems and Programs in Nine Countries* (N.Y. State School of Industrial and Labor Relations, Cornell University, 1978) is quite handy. To get a feel for the range of issues concerning working class women and their own opinions, try *Second Class, Working Class: An International Women's Reader* (Up Press, 1979). Two provocative studies on women in Soviet-type socialist countries are H. Scott, *Does Socialism Liberate Women?* (Beacon Press, 1974), and G. Lapidus, *Women in Soviet Society* (University of California Press, 1978). On China, C. Broyelle's *Women's Liberation in China* (Humanities, 1977) is rather unique, since it focuses on the question of housework, family, and sexuality in Maoist China. R. Sidel's books also focus on women's issues quite concretely. Two good collections of essays on women and modernization should also be mentioned: Wellesley Editorial Committee, *Women and National Development: The Complexities of Change* (University of Chicago Press, 1977), and I. Tinker and M. Bramsen, eds., *Women and World Development* (Overseas Development Council, 1976). Finally, a recent paperback by C. Adams and K. Winston, *Mothers at Work: Public Policies in the United States, Sweden and China* (Longman, 1980) is highly recommended.

Notes

1. R. Blumberg, "Fairy Tales and Facts: Economy, Family, Fertility and the Female," *in* I. Tinkler and M. Bramsen, eds., *Women and World Development,* p. 18.

2. B. Ehrenreich and A. Fuentes, "Life on the Global Assembly Line," *Ms,* January 1981, p. 55.

3. E. Boserup, *Woman's Role in Economic Development,* p. 33.

4. This estimate is from a business magazine, *Business Asia,* quoted by B. Ehrenreich and A. Fuentes, p. 54.

5. *Ibid,* p. 54.

6. *Ibid,* p. 55.

7. *Ibid.*

8. "Malaysian Malady: When the Spirit Hits, A Scapegoat Suffers," *Wall Street Journal* 3/7/80.

9. *Ibid.*

10. B. Ehrenreich and A. Fuentes, p. 56.

11. P. Huston, *Third World Women Speak Out,* p. 22.

12. *Ibid,* p. 20.

13. For details, see C. Adams and K. Winston, *Mothers at Work: Public Policies in the United States, Sweden and China,* p. 77.

14. L. Yanina, "Only Romeos!" *Literaturnaia gazeta,* May 12, 1971, p. 12; translated in CDSP 23, no. 24 (1971):28, quoted in G. Lapidus, *Women in Soviet Society,* p. 273.

15. E. Marok, *Literatunaia gazeta,* December 19, 1973, p. 13, quoted in G. Lapidus, *Women in Soviet Society,* p. 276.

16. Quoted in C. Broyelle, *Women's Liberation in China,* p. 80.

17. Quoted in E. Croll, *Feminism and Socialism in China,* p. 267.

18. *Ibid,* p. 273.

19. *Ibid,* pp. 272, 273.

20. G. Lapidus, *Women in Soviet Society,* p. 258.

21. A. Cook, *The Working Mother: A Survey of Problems and Programs in Nine Countries,* p. x.

22. *Ibid,* p. ix.

The Outlook for the Future

At first glance, it might seem rather presumptuous to discuss the outlook for the future of women. Soothsaying went out with the Romans and crystal balls are not the tools of the trade of the average professor. Yet the temptation to extend our analysis into the future is irresistible. We must be careful, however, to separate our fantasies from our forecasting. Each of us may nurture and express our own version of paradise. For many of us, this would be a sex-blind society, where sexual stereotypes would no longer prevent men or women from realizing their humanity. Others might find this utopia uninteresting or irrelevant. Fantasies are ultimately quite personal; they say more about the individual than about social transformation. So here we shall try to do some forecasting instead. We have already looked back over the history of women's labor in America and we have examined the current status of women and work. Now we want to see what trends and tendencies may develop further in the years ahead.

The Toll of the Triple Work Burden

The most fundamental insight from this study of women's work is that society still depends on women's productive labor in three essential areas: childbearing work, household work, and labor market

199

work. The stress of combining all three productive activities takes a toll on women's physical and mental health. Recent studies indicate that the suicide rate for white women in areas where there is a large proportion of women working is significantly high. Experts blame this high female suicide rate on role stress, especially

> *... in a period of social change in which expectations for the role performance of a working married woman as a "breadwinner" are not as clearly defined as they are for the role of wife or mother.*[1]

Apart from suicide, women have developed a severe substance abuse problem: there are an estimated 2 million women in America who are dependent on prescription drugs. In 1975, 80% of all amphetamine prescriptions, 67% of all tranquilizers, and 60% of all barbituate/sedative drugs were prescribed for women.[2] A recent government report warned:

> *One of the major health problems faced by women is that of depression. There are 175 women hospitalized because of depression to every 100 men and 238 women receive outpatient treatment to every 100 men.*[3]

The report concludes its analysis of this mental health problem with a rather unusual recommendation. It urges the economic system to provide better jobs for women:

> *The resultant increase in income would reduce the impact of life stress and raise the self-concept of women on a scale not possible through remedial psychotherapies.*[4]

In other words, the way to alleviate stress on women is *not* to *remove* women from their labor market work, but to help women achieve their rightful access to the better jobs in the labor market.

The Two-Career Family Versus the Nuclear Family

Yet the prospects for easing women's triple burden do not look bright. A recent symposium focused on the problems of the "dual-career family," the family where both spouses pursue substantially involving careers. Participants seemed to agree that the traditional nuclear, one-career family was well suited to the promotion of the husband's career and that:

A wife at home, who protects her husband's time so that it is not "frittered away" by such responsibilities, becomes an absolute necessity.[5]

They found that this one-career family was actually a two-person, one-career family, since the wife was expected to be a pseudo-employee as well. Particularly in military, political, diplomatic, church, and executive careers, the wife's participation was a prerequisite for the husband's success. For instance:

. . . some corporations encourage wives to do volunteer work in the community, fostering community welfare while at the same time promoting the public image of the firm.[6]

While many people think that this two-person, one-career pattern has faded with the entry of women into careers of their own, the conference participants were far less sanguine about the prospects for the two-career family. The new two-career family faces powerful centrifugal forces, they warn, as both spouses pursue open-ended work commitments. While they hope that greater availability of part-time work, paternity and maternity leave, and lower workloads will ease this problem, they are quite pessimistic. On the question of part-time careers or shared jobs, they note:

. . . it is more rational for a corporation to employ one person who is willing to put in a 70-hour workweek (and perhaps has a wife who works part-time on his job as well) than to employ two persons who will each work 35 hours (or less) for double the pay and fringe benefits.[7]

The problem, they are saying, is not a normative one: many husbands and wives would like to work out an egalitarian family life. The barriers are more structural:

Organizations are unlikely to take on the cost of changing existing arrangements as long as they maintain their advantageous position vis à vis labor supply. As a result of the baby boom, the professional labor market is now clogged with new entrants . . . as the baby boom generation is completing its education the pressure is now falling on the labor market. Economic recession exacerbates the problems which these youth are experiencing in finding suitable work and attaining their career objectives.[8]

Given the rigid demands of the business world and the stress this imposes on marriages, the conference participants found it "unrealistic" to expect people to remain in traditional-style marriages. Instead, they predict the continuation of trends toward later child-bearing, increased single living, higher divorce rates, and more of what they call "temporary marriages."

Business's Adjustment to the Needs of the Two-Career Family

While everyone may not agree with their pessimistic predictions on women's career-versus-family problem, the symposium participants *do* remind us that the problem is not simply whether women want careers and whether their husbands are supportive. The problem may ultimately lie with the business world, which has found the traditional family structure a very useful way of mobilizing both the husband's work input and the energies of his wife.

Assuming the business community wants or is forced to respond to the two-career family in a more progressive fashion, how might it go about this? On the one hand, some businesses have tried to make adjustments to certain inconveniences. Many firms, for instance, have taken a more understanding approach to the problem of geographical mobility, no longer demanding that their junior executives automatically move to new cities or countries as a prerequisite for corporate advancement. This has certainly eased the strains on some two-career marriages. Other firms have tried to intervene in family-versus-career problems more directly, by running "humanistic psychology" seminars at the workplace.[9] These include so-called deep-sensing seminars, characterized as no-holds-barred discussions between executives and employees.[10] Women are supposed to learn from these consultants how to combine work and family, how to decide when to have a baby, how to organize their housework, and so forth. This "advice" is tailored to the needs of the employers, who monitor the contents and results of these programs closely. Business promotes programs such as these to increase the flexibility of women's work burdens (and to increase their input into women's decisions concerning their options).

Discrimination Is Still Systemic

While it appears that women's triple burden—childbearing work, housework, and labor market work—will remain the central problem in the future, there are other problems in women's current situation that also seem to persist. The fundamental problem of discrimination against women was not eliminated in the 1960s and 1970s and may become more severe again in the 1980s and onward. As we have seen from our earlier examination of wages and occupational segregation, women still earn far less than men and substantial pressures still confine women to "pink-collar ghettos." Discrimination is still systemic. Recent data on our educational institutions, for instance, reveal that 50.6% of all instructors in public and private institutions are women, but only 9.5% of all professors are women.[11] Not only are these findings personally disturbing to women in academia, they should be cause for concern to anyone who thinks that the values and ideals of future generations are learned in the classrooms of today. The next generation of students may be relearning the same sex stereotypes that reinforce sex discrimination.

Unfortunately, the "regulatory reformers" of the Reagan administration "are quietly planning a major relaxation of government rules aimed at preventing discrimination against minorities in employment. . ." with "new rules reducing the number of companies covered by affirmative action requirements."[12] At the Equal Employment Opportunity Commission, "the backlog of cases has been growing, and this will be exacerbated by the $20 million budget cut proposed by Reagan."[13] As the government dismantles the civil rights machinery, it will become more difficult for women (and minorities) to fight discrimination in the future.

Brighter Prospects: Women Unionizing

Women's future may not be entirely bleak. As the government abandons its equal employment opportunity programs, women will probably continue their shift into the union movement, since relations between women and the unions have rarely been more cordial than now. This will undoubtedly improve the union movement, infusing it with new blood and more creative tactics. It will also mean workplace-based support for large numbers of working women and some wage benefits as well. Optimism on this front seems well founded.

Desexing the Job Structure

There are also some interesting developments on the horizon with respect to the sex-stereotyping of jobs. As noted earlier, women have begun to infiltrate certain traditionally male jobs, although this progress has been slow, particularly for the "elite" jobs such as corporate executives or tenured professors. Men, however, seem to be entering some of the traditionally pink-collar jobs with surprising speed. From 1972 to 1978, the number of male secretaries rose 24%, the number of male telephone operators increased 38%, and the number of male nurses increased 94%.[14] Why? Experts seem to agree that a major reason men are moving into these jobs is that traditionally male blue-collar jobs are decreasing. As the economy continues its shift toward service sector work, men will have to follow women into the service sector jobs. Furthermore, the younger generation of men entering the work force may have less rigid notions about what constitutes women's work, which would encourage them to try some formerly female occupations.

The men's experiences on these jobs are quite mixed. Some studies find these nontraditional males engendering more hostility than nontraditional females:

> *Male nursing students are rated as unattractive, unrealistic, and unambitious. The results suggest that men entering a predominantly female profession may be perceived as more deviant than women entering a predominantly male profession.*[15]

Others find the reverse:

> *. . . men who now go into nursing get preferential treatment from hospital administrators, and from traditional females within the hospital milieu even though they may be discriminated against by some of the individual female nurses. Administrators in general tend to prefer advancement for males.*[16]

Eventually, much of the controversy and excitement over these avant-garde men will cool down. But when the dust has settled, some more fundamental changes will be clear. The status, the wages, and the working conditions in these formerly female jobs will improve. As one male nurse commented:

> *"Guys get together and organize and are willing to fight for more. . . . Once we get a 30% or 40% ratio of men in nursing you'll see salaries and the whole status of the job improve."*[17]

While the secular shortage of nurses or secretaries would raise wages in these fields anyway, as males integrate female trades they should push the entire wage scale upwards. So far this has not happened. The average female clerical wage in 1979 was $10,347, compared to the male average of $16,729.[18] Apart from the wage question, bosses do not give their male secretaries the menial chores they used to ask women to do routinely. As one man noted:

... his boss asked him for coffee the first day on the job—and never again in more than two years. "It must have struck some chord in him to see me waiting on him. . . ."[19]

Again, it is unclear whether male entry into the female trades will really improve conditions for women workers, but the outlook seems hopeful.

Self-Employed Women on the Rise

One of the least sensational but most promising developments for women in the future may be self-employment. While the absolute number of self-employed women is still small, the relative number is growing steadily. The percentage of self-employed women (of all employed women) rose from 4.4% in 1970 to 4.9% in 1979.[20] Although this may seem to be a modest increase, the age distribution has shifted significantly. In 1970, the median age of the self-employed woman was 47.8; by 1979 it was 42.7, with the big increase in the 25- to 34-year-old group.[21] These self-employed women are engaged in a variety of businesses, from the mundane to the spectacular. There are the free-lance inventors and writers as well as the more straight-forward businesses, ranging from banks to record companies. Of course, not all of these businesses are all-female or feminist, but they do offer a growing number of women the satisfaction of trying out their ideas, without unnecessary sexual interference. While self-employment is difficult financially, it may provide women with some needed autonomy in the future.

The Computerized Future

Our overall outlook for women is rather mixed. Certain problems, such as the triple burden and discrimination, seem structurally embedded in our society, with small potential for improvement unless some more fundamental changes take place. There are bright-er prospects in certain areas, particularly in pink-collar work and in self-employment. It is still important, though, to situate the outlook for women within the more general context of the future of our industrial society.

According to professional futurists, we will all (male and female) have to live with the computer revolution. Office workers have already been forced to cope with the new technology of word pro-cessors and video display terminals. But the futurists predict that the biggest impact of the computer revolution will be to move the office back to the home. Homes of the future will be "electronic cottages" with computer terminals that will make remote-control work possible. Families will be reunited again in household production, using home terminals to do their work (and to shop and provide entertainment).[22]

While at present this cottage industry concept is restricted to the workaholic executives who want to work longer hours at home after a day at the office, the futurists expect it to become more widespread in the future. The implications for women workers and the double burden are ambiguous. Will this become the new way to combine work and family? Ironically, one *Business Week* editor wondered where the family would even come from in this scenario, since there would seem to be so few social contacts left in this futuristic world.[23]

Business futurists are indeed predicting a bizarre world for all of us. It is important to realize that women will play a pivotal role in these scenarios. Even now, women are employed producing the technology that will make this future possible. And, as the core of the office labor force in America, women will carry out the most critical implementation phase of the information processing revolution. While robotic automation has already been integrated into assembly line work (replacing many women workers), the critical battlefield will probably be in the office. When the office is conquered by information processing systems, management will be revolutionized and the door will be open to the electronic cottages of the future.

Since women's work is critical to this process, women can expect to be the target of business's interest in the next few years. Guidance sessions on the job will be more sophisticated, with more advice about balancing work and family duties. The popular media may perfect their "new woman" prototype: assertiveness trained, dressed for success, timing her childbearing to minimize career disruption. In the distant future, surrogate mothering may even eliminate this problem. The traditional nuclear family may fall by the wayside as business learns to accommodate its marketing strategy to singles living alone. As one marketing expert remarked recently:

> *"There is nothing in this that business would be opposed to. People living alone need the same things as people living in families. The difference is there's no sharing. So really this trend is good because it means you sell more products."*[24]

Regardless of whether women in America *want* this kind of society, we must think about it quite seriously. The business community has already studied *its* future needs and interests, and designed its strategies accordingly. Can women afford to do anything less?

Notes

1. J. Newman, K. Whittermore, and H. Newman, "Women in the Labor Force and Suicide," *Social Problems,* 1973, 21(2), p. 227.

2. From the Report of the Special Populations Subpanel on Mental Health of Women, submitted to the President's Advisory Commission on Mental Health, quoted in *Voices for Women,* 1980, Report of the President's Advisory Committee for Women, 1980, p. 59.

3. *Ibid,* p. 58.

4. *Ibid,* p. 59. (It is remarkable for a mental health study to urge workplace justice over increased mental health treatment.)

5. J. Mortimer, "Dual Career Families—A Sociological Perspective," *in* S. Peterson, J. Richardson, and G. Kreuter, eds., *The Two-Career Family: Issues and Alternatives,* p. 5.

6. *Ibid.*

7. *Ibid,* p. 17.

8. *Ibid,* p. 18.

9. See "Employees Get Help on Delicate Balance of Work and Family," *Wall Street Journal* 4/3/80.

10. See "Deep Sensing: A Pipeline to Employee Morale," *Business Week,* January 29, 1979.

11. Data for 1979, from the National Center for Education Statistics, quoted in *Voices for Women,* p. 39.

12. "Rewriting the Job-Bias Rules," *Business Week,* April 13, 1981, p. 177.

13. *Ibid.*

14. From an Urban Institute study quoted in "More Men Infiltrating Professions Historically Dominated by Women," *Wall Street Journal* 2/25/81.

15. S. Hesselbart, "Women Doctors Win and Male Nurses Lose," *Sociology of Work and Occupations,* Vol. 4, # 1, February 1977, pp. 49–62.

16. "The Male Sister: Sexual Separation of Labor in Society," by H. Etzkowitz, *Journal of Marriage and the Family,* August 1971, p. 433.

17. Quoted in "More Men Infiltrating Professions Historically Dominated by Women," *Wall Street Journal,* 2/25/81.

18. C. Doudna, "Male Secretaries: New Men of Letters," *New York Times Magazine,* April 5, 1981, p. 134.

19. *Ibid,* p. 123.

20. U.S. Department of Labor, *Perspectives on Working Women: A Data Book,* Bulletin 2080, October 1980, p. 13.

21. *Ibid.*

22. See A. Toffler, *The Third Wave,* or C. Evans, *The Micro Millennium.*

23. "Do We Want Machines That Can Outthink Us?" *Business Week,* April 21, 1980.

24. Quoted in B. Ehrenreich and D. English, *For Her Own Good* (Anchor Press, Doubleday: 1978), p. 262.

Index